EDITED BY **NIKOLAU**

BEYOND BLESSINGS

Celebrating the Joys of Stewardship

Pacific Press®
Publishing Association

Nampa, Idaho | Oshawa, Ontario, Canada
www.pacificpress.com

Stewardship Sermon Contest Winners

This book contains

the 12 winning stewardship sermons

Sponsored by

Stewardship Ministries

North American Division of Seventh-day Adventists

John Mathews, Director

Co-Sponsored by

Ministerial Department

North American Division
of Seventh-day Adventists
Ivan L. Williams Sr., Director

Ministry

International Journal for Pastors
Derek Morris, Editor

Cover design by Gerald Lee Monks
Cover design resources from iStockphoto.com
Inside design by Kristin Hansen-Mellish

The authors assume full responsibility for the accuracy of all facts and quotations as cited in this book.

Scriptures quoted from CEV are from the Contemporary English Version, Copyright © American Bible Society 1991, 1995. Used by permission.

Scripture quotations marked ESV are from The Holy Bible, English Standard Version® (ESV®), copyright © 2001 by Crossway, a publishing ministry of Good News Publishers. Used by permission. All rights reserved.

Scripture quotations marked ISV are taken from the Holy Bible: International Standard Version®. Copyright © 1996-2013 by The ISV Foundation. ALL RIGHTS RESERVED INTERNATIONALLY. Used by permission.

Scripture quotations from *The Message*. Copyright © by Eugene H. Peterson, 1993, 1994, 1995. Used by permission of NavPress Publishing Group.

Scripture quotations marked NASB are taken from *The New American Standard Bible®*, Copyright © 1960, 1962, 1963, 1968, 1971, 1972, 1973, 1975, 1977, 1995 by The Lockman Foundation. Used by permission.

Scripture quotations marked NIV are from the HOLY BIBLE, NEW INTERNATIONAL VERSION®. Copyright © 1973, 1978, 1984 by International Bible Society. Used by permission of Zondervan Publishing House. All rights reserved.

Scripture quotations marked NKJV are from The New King James Version, copyright © 1979, 1980, 1982, Thomas Nelson, Inc., Publishers.

Scripture quotations marked NLT are taken from the Holy Bible, New Living Translation, copyright ©1996, 2004, 2007. Used by permission of Tyndale House Publishers, Inc., Carol Stream, Illinois 60188. All Rights Reserved.

Scriptures quoted from Phillips are from J. B. Phillips: The New Testament in Modern English, Revised Edition, copyright © J. B. Phillips 1958, 1960, 1972.Used by permission of Macmillan Publishing Co., Inc.

Additional copies of this book are available by calling toll-free 1-800-765-6955 or by visiting http://www.adventistbookcenter.com.

Library of Congress Cataloging-in-Publication Data:

Beyond blessings : celebrating the joys of stewardship / Editor,
Nikolaus Satelmajer. Contributors, C. Adelina Alexe ... [et al.].
    pages cm
  ISBN 13: 978-0-8163-4509-0 (pbk.)
  ISBN 10: 0-8163-4509-0 (pbk.)
  1. Christian stewardship—Sermons. 2. Seventh-day
Adventists—Sermons. I. Satelmajer, Nikolaus, 1944–
  BV772.B45 2013
  248'.6–dc23
                 2013010515

13 14 15 16 17 • 5 4 3 2 1

Editor:

Nikolaus Satelmajer

Contributors:

C. Adelina Alexe, David L. Bissell, G. Tom Carter, Gerry Christman, Ernest Dobkins, Daniel B. Martella, Jeff Metherell, Domingo Paulino, Orlando Rosales, Robin Song, Patrick Vincent, Harold O. White

Contents

Introduction   9

Contributors   12

Where Your Heart Belongs   17
C. Adelina Alexe

Guaranteed Returns   27
David L. Bissell

Multiplying and Unifying the Church Through Stewardship   37
G. Tom Carter

Called to Share   47
Gerry Christman

Those Mighty Mites   57
Ernest Dobkins

Investing in Heaven   65
Daniel B. Martella

"X" Marks the Spot   73
Jeff Metherell

Knowledge, Commitment, and Transformation—the Making of a
Faithful Steward   83
Domingo Paulino

Trusting God   93
Orlando Rosales

Does God Need My Money?   101
Robin Song

Why We Bring the Tithe   109
Patrick Vincent

Can't Buy Love   119
Harold O. White

Introduction

My wife, Ruth, and I met each other in New York City and, not too long after, married. Before getting married, we visited different congregations to see which church we would make our home. We decided on a new church—the Manhattan Seventh-day Adventist Church.

Each Sabbath we traveled by subway to 232 West 11th Street in what is known as Greenwich Village. The members gathered from all sections of the city, and even from outside New York City. Years later, we enjoy reflecting on our time in that congregation and still keep in contact with some of the members.

One of the families I remember was a young couple with five children. During the worship service, the deacons needed just a little extra time to receive the tithe and offering envelopes from this family. The family did not place just *one* envelope into the offering plate—*each* child deposited an envelope. Deliberately and carefully, each child placed an envelope into the offering plate. The children relished the experience, though the amount they gave was but a token of what the membership as a whole gave. The act of depositing the tithe and offering envelope was important to the children, and the deacons waited graciously. Let's face it—if you enjoy doing something, you want to prolong the experience. This scene is still vivid in my mind; I learned much about stewardship from those children. Stewardship is personal, enjoyable, and repeatable.

Twelve sermons—One message

This book is a collection of twelve stewardship sermons. These sermons are the winning sermons of a stewardship contest open to ministers and graduate ministerial students throughout the North American Division—Bermuda, Canada, and the United States. Each sermon gives a different perspective on stewardship, yet you will find certain themes in all of them.

This collection of stewardship sermons is the fulfillment of a desire to provide needed resources to congregations by John Mathews, stewardship director, North American Division of Seventh-day Adventists. Ivan L. Williams Sr., ministerial director of the North American Division, and Derek Morris, editor of *Ministry,* gave their enthusiastic support to the search for quality stewardship sermons. At Pacific Press®, we owe thanks to Jerry D. Thomas, Douglas Church, and their teams for their part in making the book an appealing and timely resource.

Helping you

The primary purpose of this book is to be a stewardship resource for local congregations. Some will find the material helpful in their study of stewardship; while others may use it for group study, such as prayer meetings. If you are asked to preach, you may use these sermons in your preaching and share the message as presented by each writer. All readers will discover helpful biblical material in the messages; but, additionally, you will find the personal experiences of the writers engaging and encouraging. These writers include theory along with personal experience—they share the blessings they have experienced as God's stewards.

It's about mission

The Seventh-day Adventist Church has always focused on mission. Even before the church was organized, individuals and groups were proclaiming the return of Jesus Christ. After it was organized, the church soon embarked on a mission to proclaim worldwide key biblical messages. Imagine—a small group of church members starting a worldwide proclamation of the return of Christ, the Sabbath, and other key biblical teachings. How could such a small body of believers grow into a movement that spans the world? In part, it was because the members were faithful stewards—they faithfully gave of their time, talents, and possessions. First, the church had individuals willing to take the message to all parts of the world. Some even gave their lives in order to fulfill this mission. Secondly, the members, through faithful tithing and sacrificial offerings for both local and international needs, supported the mission of the church. Think about this—the church in which you worship did not always exist. How did it start? Someone had a vision to plant a congregation. Many people, no doubt, gave sacrificially. In fact, most likely, people in distant places contributed to establish the church where you worship. The Seventh-day Adventist system of sharing tithe and offerings to fulfill our mission is one of the reasons this movement is truly a worldwide movement. Stewardship and mission belong together.

Stewardship is one way we define our relationship with God. God invited Adam and Eve to be faithful stewards, and He invites *us* to be faithful stewards. How will you and I respond to that invitation? Are we willing to step forward and respond to God's invitation? If we trust God, we will willingly and enthusiastically respond to Him.

God blesses us with time, talents, and possessions. How we use the time, talents, and possessions defines the kind of stewards we are.

Nikolaus Satelmajer
Silver Spring, Maryland, U.S.A.

Contributors

Cristina Adelina Alexe, is a PhD student with an emphasis in systematic theology and New Testament studies at the Seventh-day Adventist Theological Seminary, Andrews University. She completed her undergraduate studies in her native Romania and earned her MDiv at Andrews University. In addition to being very active in the churches she has attended, she also worked in several countries. She was an English teacher in China and an elementary teacher in Palau.

David L. Bissell, has been a pastor, Bible teacher, guidance counselor, college professor, and recently retired as a pastor in the Iowa-Missouri Conference of Seventh-day Adventists. While he spent most of his career in the United States, he spent eight years in Asia, teaching in South Korea and Hong Kong. He obtained his education at several colleges and universities, earning his DMin from the Seventh-day Adventist Theological Seminary, Andrews University. One of his personal interests is music—singing, saxophone, and guitar.

G. Tom Carter, received his BA in religion from Union College and, after pastoring for eleven years, studied law and received his JD degree from Emory University School of Law. For fifty-five years, he has used his pastoral and legal training in various capacities in the Seventh-day Adventist Church. For twenty-five years he was the trust director of the General Conference of Seventh-day Adventists and, currently, is the trust director of the Southern Union Conference of Seventh-day Adventists.

Gerry D. Christman, has been a pastor, academy teacher, theology professor, and college president. Part of his career was at Chile Adventist University in Chile and Northeast Brazil College in Brazil. Currently, he is the pastor of the Aiea Seventh-day Adventist Church, Hawaii. He earned his BA from Southwestern Adventist University and his MDiv and DMin degrees from the Seventh-day Adventist Theological Seminary at Andrews University. Additionally, he received his MPH degree from Loma Linda University.

Ernest Dobkins, after studying laboratory techniques, served as a missionary at Hospital Bella Vista, Puerto Rico. After he received a BA in theology from Andrews University, he was a pastor in Minnesota and Texas. He studied trust work at California State University and received the designation of certified specialist in planned giving. Before retiring, he worked in trust services for the Seventh-day Adventist conferences in Minnesota, Texas, Rocky Mountain, and Northern California. He still works part time with the Northern California Conference of Seventh-day Adventists.

Daniel B. Martella, has been a camp counselor, student literature evangelist, and pastor. One of his pastoral roles emphasized secular campus ministries in Chico, California. While a college student, he spent one year as a student missionary at the Seventh-day Adventist language school in Pusan, South Korea. He received his BA degree in theology from Pacific Union College and his MDiv from the Seventh-day Adventist Theological

Seminary at Andrews University. Currently, he is the pastor of the Healdsburg and Cloverdale Seventh-day Adventist churches in northern California.

Jeff Metherell, is director of stewardship, planned giving and trust services, and religious liberty departments of the Wisconsin Conference of Seventh-day Adventists. Previously, he was an account executive with several mortgage companies in Colorado and California. He was also manager of medical staff relations and similar positions. A graduate of Walla Walla University (BA), he studied law at the University of Denver Sturm College of Law, where he received his JD degree.

Domingo A. Paulino, has been a literature evangelist and pastor in New York, California, and North Carolina. Currently, he is the pastor of the Durham and Raleigh Spanish Seventh-day Adventist churches. Additionally, he is responsible for three Spanish groups in Sanford, Henderson, and Carrboro. A graduate of Antillean Adventist University (BA), he received his MDiv and DMin degrees from the Seventh-day Adventist Theological Seminary, Andrews University.

Orlando Jose Rosales, has been a pastor, evangelist, and conference administrator in Venezuela and the United States. Currently, he pastors the Baltimore and Dundalk Spanish Seventh-day Adventist churches and also serves as assistant director of multilingual ministries for the Chesapeake Conference of Seventh-day Adventists. He graduated from

Colombia University (BA), Montemorelos University (MA), and currently is part of the DMin program at Andrews University.

Robin Song, is the English ministry pastor for the Living Vine Fellowship/Seattle Central Korean Seventh-day Adventist Church in Washington State. Previously, he pastored in New York and Illinois. He graduated from the University of Toronto with a degree in applied science and received ministerial training at the Seventh-day Adventist Theological Seminary, Andrews University, where he received his MDiv degree.

Patrick E. Vincent, a senior pastor of the Mount Calvary Seventh-day Adventist Church, Tampa, Florida. Previously, he pastored congregations in the southeastern parts of the United States. A graduate of West Indies College (BA), he received his MDiv degree from the Seventh-day Adventist Theological Seminary, Andrews University. He also received a DMin degree from Vanderbilt University Divinity School.

Harold White, was drafted into the U.S. Army and served for eighteen months in Germany. After completing his military service, he was a computer programmer, at which time he became a Seventh-day Adventist. Upon graduation from Union College (BA), he started his ministry at the College View Seventh-day Adventist Church in Lincoln, Nebraska. Following his pastoral ministry in several states, he serves as the administrative pastor of the Sacramento Central Seventh-day Adventist Church.

Where Your Heart Belongs

C. Adelina Alexe

Seated with the disciples gathered around Him on the shore of the Galilee Sea, Jesus delivered what we often refer to as the "Sermon on the Mount" (Matthew 5–7). Even though the Greek word describing the location is that for mountain, some commentators suggest that the mountain was actually a hill north or west of the Lake of Galilee, where the hills rise steeply from the lake. In this sermon, one writer states, Jesus addresses "a Christian's character, influence, righteousness, piety, goals and priorities, relationships, and commitment."[1]

Let us read Matthew 6:19–21 together, out loud.

> "Do not lay up for yourselves treasures on earth, where moth and rust destroy and where thieves break in and steal; but lay up for yourselves treasures in heaven, where neither moth nor rust destroys and where thieves do not break in and steal. For where your treasure is, there your heart will be also" (Matthew 6:19–21, NKJV).

One of the features in this passage is the inverse parallel-ism in verses 19 and 20, where one of the sentences describes the opposite of the other. The word *but* in verse 19 puts us on notice that what follows is different from what comes before it. If we reduce the phrase to its core structure, we read: "Do not lay up treasures on earth, but lay up treasures in heaven." The almost identical wording underscores the contrast between the key words *earth* and *heaven,* indicating that this passage is really a comparison between heaven and earth.

Jesus invites us to store up treasures in heaven, not on earth, and the reason why we should do so is found in the explanation following the word *where:*

> "Do not lay up for yourselves treasures on earth, where moth and rust destroy and where thieves break in and steal; but lay up for your-selves treasures in heaven, where neither moth nor rust destroys and where thieves do not break in and steal" (verses 19, 20).

To help us understand why we should not store up trea-sures on earth, but in heaven, Jesus describes heaven and earth. He does so quite fascinatingly, in only three words: *moth, rust,* and *thieves.* Let's take a closer look at each of these and see what they reveal.

Moth

Most of us know what a moth is, right? Those tiny crea-tures that can create unwanted new patterns in your carpet, or turn your sweater into an unexpected piece of art. As a friend of mine put it, they are the "not-quite-as-cool-as-a-butterfly insect." This is the picture that usually comes to my mind whenever I read this passage. The truth is, though, I have never seen a moth. The fact that Jesus spoke of the moth sparked my curiosity about this somewhat evasive insect. What I discovered surprised me.

Listen to this description of a moth. "A moth is an insect related to the butterfly, both being of the order Lepidoptera. Most of this order are moths; there are thought to be about 160,000 species of moth . . . , with thousands of species yet to be described."[2] What's intriguing about moths is that, it seems most—if not all—species are pests. They cause damage. They are agents of destruction, and not only of carpets and coats. Corn borer and bollworm caterpillars damage the ears of corn, as well as the stalks, by chewing tunnels, which cause the plants to fall over. In many parts of the world, they are a major agricultural pest. The diamondback moth is a serious pest on cabbage, cauliflower, and so on. The caterpillar of the gypsy moth causes severe damage to forests. There is also the codling moth that causes extensive damage to fruit farms. The larvae of Tineidae moths eat clothes and blankets made from natural fibers such as wool, silk, fur, or feathers.

Moths are truly agents of destruction for fruits and vegetables (our food), trees (our environment), and clothes. What really struck me as I discovered these facts was the breadth of harm Jesus grasped in just one word—*moth*. Even years after Jesus chose the moth to describe destruction, we still understand what He had in mind.

Rust

Jesus also refers to rust. "In colloquial usage, the term is applied to red oxides, formed by the reaction of iron and oxygen in the presence of water or air moisture."[3]

Those of us especially living in northern climates are familiar with rust on our cars. Car rust can be a problem, but we don't typically think of it in terms of disaster. Rust, however, has the potential to put us in great peril, as the story of the collapse of the Mianus River Bridge in Connecticut shows. On June 28, 1983, the bridge failed when the bearings rusted internally and pushed one corner of the road slab off its support.

Rust was also an important factor in the Silver Bridge disaster of 1967 in West Virginia, when a steel suspension bridge collapsed in less than a minute. Forty-six people lost their lives. The bridge failure was due to a defect in a single link.[4] "A small crack was formed through fretting wear at the bearing, and grew through internal corrosion. . . . The crack was only about 0.1 inch deep when it went critical, and it broke in a brittle fashion. . . . When the lower side of the eyebar failed, all the load was transferred to the other side of the eyebar, which then failed by ductile overload. . . . The chain was completely severed. Collapse of the entire structure was inevitable since all parts of a suspension bridge are in equilibrium with one another."[5] After the disaster, the Silver Bridge was sometimes referred to as "a monster of death."

In art and literature, rust has been used as a metaphor for ruin, decay, and faded glory. Jesus' use of the word makes no exception. The breadth of what He covered in this one word clearly points to decay—we understand what He said.

But there is another aspect to rust. It can also be a plant disease affecting leaves, stems, fruits, and seeds. Plant rusts are parasites and require a living host, such as a plant, to complete their life cycle. Cereal crops can be devastated in one season, and trees often die due to this.

So moths and rust affect our accommodation and commodities, means of transportation, food, environment, and clothes. This covers a significant part of our lives, doesn't it?

Thieves

Although condemned in the Bible and prohibited by law, stealing has infested our world with much loss and grief, generating an atmosphere of insecurity and anxiety. Stealing takes place in different ways, at various levels, and with a diverse range of targets. Individuals, organizations, governments, and nations can steal. One can seek to appropriate for himself or herself someone else's material goods, intellectual property, or identity. Adultery involves coveting and stealing someone else's spouse. Innocence and dignity can be stolen. We can steal someone else's time, efforts, identity, and talents. We can steal someone's present, and rob them of their future.

Again, one word, the one concept Jesus chose to illustrate the human decay, is broad and easily understood. The word describes the condition of the entire human race—selfishness. It is, indeed, selfishness that stands at the foundation of sin. Lucifer wanted to steal God's throne. Eve and Adam stole each other's innocence and robbed all their descendants of God's presence and the peace of a sinless heart. Selfishness has marked and driven the course of human beings who are bound for decay and, eventually, complete destruction.

What is heaven like?

Jesus' words are remarkably rich in content and meaning. They are a carefully crafted summary of all evil on earth. Natural and moral evil are terms that generally describe two types of evil. Natural evil refers to evil in the material and animal world not caused by human beings, while moral evil describes the evil caused by humans. In Matthew 6:19, 20, Jesus encompasses the reality of all evil through three words that represent the three types of evil on earth:

> Moth: representing animal natural evil
> Rust: representing material natural evil
> Thieves: representing human moral evil

In three words, He clearly sums up the condition of our planet with all it contains and illustrates the heart of His teaching: earthly life is marked by instability and insecurities and saturated with the pain of loss and separation. Yet, this passage reveals not only the decay characteristic of our fallen planet, but also a solution, an alternative to perishing. As

One who came down from heaven, the Son of God goes on to weave hope into the reality of the world He just depicted. It is now time to lift our eyes towards the land of the redeemed.

We often think of the afterlife and wonder what it will be like. Even among Christians who read the Bible, there are various ideas about what heaven is like. Let's see what kind of heaven this biblical passage reveals to us:

1. Heaven, like earth, is real and yet distinct from earth. Have you heard people say that heaven is what we make of our lives on earth? That is a nice way to suggest that being loving, good, and responsible during our lives here can help us make a little heaven in our lives and the lives of others. However, heaven is the name for something that is actually real and distinct from earth. To neglect the reality of heaven and the physical distinction between heaven and earth is to forego much of what the Bible has to say, sadly to our loss.

2. Evil—natural or moral—will not exist in heaven; therefore, no loss. On earth everything is unstable, uncertain, and insecure; it is subject to decay, destruction, stealing, and loss. Heaven is the opposite: everything is eternal, durable, secure, and imperishable. In heaven, there is no loss.

In the past two centuries, the theory of evolution has gained wide acceptance, even among many Christians. When a Christian accepts evolution, though, he or she inevitably agrees that evil existed before the Fall, since animal death is supposed to have occurred before the creation of humans. Because a Christian who believes in evolution needs to reject a literal fall of Adam and Eve and redefine sin, the certainty of our future is also dismantled into mere opinions, some optimistic, some rather pessimistic. But Matthew 6:19, 20 points out that evil—all evil—will not characterize the world of the redeemed.

3. Heaven is something we should wish for. Jesus invites us to lay up treasures for ourselves in heaven. Heaven is something we should wish for, and only we can choose for ourselves. It is not something we can give up so others can have it; Jesus made provision for everyone who desires it. But in these verses Jesus appeals to us personally. The heaven we discover in Matthew 6:19, 20 is a real place, distinct from earth, where no evil exists, where no loss of any kind will occur. But, of what value or relevance would it be for us to know that such a beautiful and happy place exists, if we could not partake of it?

4. Heaven is possible to attain. The most hopeful part in all of what Jesus is saying is that we *can* have part in this reward. The very One whose hands and feet were pierced with iron nails so we can partake of heaven, invites us to lay up treasures there even while living on earth.

But how are we to gather treasures in heaven? We cannot fly there to lay up gold or goods, and we don't have a bank of heaven where we can store our money to keep it safe. R. T. France reminds us that heavenly treasures are "stored up not by my performing meritorious acts, but by belonging to and living by the priorities of the kingdom of heaven."[6]

Ellen White fills in the contours of what "heavenly treasure" means: "Every opportunity to help a brother in need, or to aid the cause of God in the spread of the truth, is a pearl that you can send beforehand, and deposit in the bank of heaven for safe keeping."[7] She also writes, "What shall we do with our time, our understanding, our possessions, which are not ours, but are entrusted to us to test our honesty? Let us bring them to Jesus. Let us use our treasures for the advancement of His cause. Thus we shall obey the injunction, 'Lay not up for yourselves treasures upon earth, . . . but lay up for yourselves treasures in heaven.' "[8]

Sometimes people suggest Jesus' words in Matthew 6 speak against wealth and well-being. The text, however, does not indicate a requirement for us to live in poverty. Rather, the word *treasure* for many implies gathering, storing up wealth. It suggests a way to create security for ourselves by relying on our own powers and resources. But, "possessed by our posses-sions, we discover that we cannot will our way free of posses-sions. Yet if we can be freed, that that is so true, so beautiful may grasp our attention, we discover we have been dispos-sessed. To seek first the righteousness of the kingdom of God is to discover that for which we seek is given, not achieved."[9]

Jesus invites us to walk through this life as people who have accepted the gift of heaven.

Conclusion

Perhaps you think you are not worthy of heaven; you've been wandering away from God, and heaven sounds like a place someone like you could not attain. You are separating yourself from the Shepherd's flock because you don't feel worthy to walk among them. Jesus calls you home. He calls you back. He calls you to be transformed, and wants you to accept the promise of heaven. You are renewed in His blood. You are a son or daughter of God, and *you* belong in heaven.

Perhaps you've been bewildered by ideas saying that heaven is not real. You've wondered about the meaning of the Bi-ble, questioned the Scripture, and doubted the truth. Please know that in Jesus, there is no deceit. God Himself engraved His Word for us to remember that heaven is real. Heaven is being prepared for you to take part in when Jesus returns to take you home. Embrace this promise. Weave it into your life goals, and let its fragrance enhance each day of your life here.

Perhaps you have been deprived of material goods that you have worked so hard to attain. I know that Jesus grieves your loss with you. He invites you to trust Him and make Him your Shelter. He is the God who can renew not only hope, but things as well. Heaven and the earth made new are promised to you. And while living with your eyes on that promised future, may the blessing and wisdom of God be your part and guide.

Perhaps you have invested your talents in reaching out to

others; you have sacrificed in ways they may never have imagined, yet your efforts don't seem to be appreciated, nor is the reward in sight. May the Spirit of Jesus move you forward in God's strength, defying discouragement and disposing of disappointment.

Perhaps the truth of a heaven where beauty is unmarred and joy is endless cannot be grasped through your tearing eyes. Maybe you've lost someone dear. Maybe you've lost hope for a loved one. Your heart may have grown heavy dealing with the sorrows of this life. Lift your eyes to the sky, breathe in the freshness of this very moment of life, and may you be reminded that heaven is a place of reunion, healing, and peace. Don't lose faith; don't lose sight; don't lose heart. And in so doing, may the peace and healing of heaven be upon you even in this very moment with strength renewed and hope restored.

Matthew 6:21 states, "For where your treasure is, there your heart will be also."

Your heart belongs to the kingdom of your Father. And that's where your treasure is.

Endnotes

1. George Knight, *The Abundant Life Bible Amplifier: Matthew* (Boise, Idaho: Pacific Press® Publishing Association, 1994), 77.

2. http://en.wikipedia.org/wiki/Moth (accessed June 30, 2012).

3. http://en.wikipedia.org/wiki/Rust (accessed July 28, 2012).

4. Ibid.

5. http://en.wikipedia.org/wiki/Silver_Bridge (accessed March 27, 2013).

6. R. T. France, *The Gospel of Matthew* (Grand Rapids, Mich.: Eerdmans Publishing Co., 2007), 259.

7. Ellen G. White, *Christian Service,* electronic edition (Silver Spring, Md.: Review and Herald® Publishing Association), 221.3.

8. Ellen G. White, *Counsels on Stewardship,* electronic edition (Silver

Spring, Md.: Review and Herald®), 116, 117.

9. Stanley Hauerwas, *Matthew* (Grand Rapids, Mich.: Brazos Press, 2007), 81.

Guaranteed Returns

David L. Bissell

Recently I visited Andrews University, my alma mater. As I meandered up the walkway into the new seminary building, my eyes were drawn to the names on the dedicatory tiles in the walkway. One name stood out, in my mind, above all others. It was Harry K. Show. He was one of the business managers of Andrews when I studied theology in the undergraduate school. I was flooded with memories of the miraculous. H. K., as many knew him, was a man with a wry smile, and yet someone who could strike terror in the hearts of students.

It was in December 1965, eight months before I was to graduate, that I was required to visit Mr. Show's office. *Why would he want to see me?* I wondered. I soon found out. I needed the $250 entrance fee before I could begin my final semester. There were no student grants available, at least none that I knew about. Real money or an additional student loan was the requirement for continuing my education. This was my crisis of faith. I had no money, no one from whom I could borrow, and I had nothing to sell. I needed to take eighteen hours one semester and nineteen the next, and a full load during the summer in order to graduate in August. Working extra hours wasn't an option. I was planning to be married in the summer, and I had an invitation to be a ministerial intern in Wisconsin. I didn't want to borrow more money. How would I ever pay back my twelve hundred dollars in student loans? Back then that was a lot of money. Everything was on the line. I walked out of the office, shaken to my very roots. What could I do?

In my mind, I went back to the beginning of the year and recalled another crisis of faith. I had a habit of reading scripture, and my meditation that day took me to Malachi 3:8–10. "Will a man rob God? Yet you are robbing me. . . . In your tithes and contributions. . . . Bring the full tithe into the storehouse.... And thereby put me to the test . . . if I will not open the windows of heaven for you and pour down for you a blessing until there is no more need" (ESV). I wished I had read another passage in the Bible that day. Somehow I had missed returning my tithe the year before, on the one thousand dollars I had earned toward my school bill. I don't even recall how I discovered this, but immediately my conscience began to bother me. But now I had a dilemma—how would I come up with one hundred dollars for the tithe I had not returned? I had sold religious books during the summer, and I needed every penny for the upcoming school year. So, I sold my car and pocketed the $150. Yes, I had the money, but I needed it for school. What if I used that money for tithe? How could I finish school? Wouldn't it be all right for me to use it for my education? After all, I was going to be a pastor. Surely it wouldn't be robbing God to use it for such a worthy cause! For two weeks I argued with myself, struggling with the dilemma. Should I, should I not . . . should I, should I not? The conflict was real, and I did not know what to do.

Finally, the thought came to me. *I'm going to be a pastor and encourage people to return a faithful tithe—if I am not a faithful tither, what good will my ministry be? I need to "test" God for myself.* The next Sabbath I placed my one hundred dollars in the offering plate, hoping against hope that God would be true to His promise. Three months passed. All of the money I had earned during the summer was gone. That is why I was sitting in Mr. Show's office now. We went over options for me to continue school. There was only one option—I needed $250 or I could not enter my final semester. Fear gripped my heart.

Rather discouraged, I walked out of H. K.'s office. The options were not appealing. Maybe I couldn't get married that summer. Who knows whether the Wisconsin Conference would hire me a year later? What would happen to me? I went to my classes that day, mulling over my future. That evening I went to bed as usual and got up early in the morning to work as a night desk manager and janitor in Burman Hall. It was my responsibility during the night to clean the showers. As I cleaned the showers, I often spent time praying as I cleaned them. That morning, my prayers were urgent. "Lord, what am I going to do? I can't go to school unless I have the funds. I think You want me to marry Jeanette. I think You want me to be a minister. I don't think You want me to borrow more money . . . Lord, I need a miracle."

As I finished my prayer, a peace settled over me. Somehow I knew God would take care of me. I didn't know how but I believed the promise. The day passed quickly and late in the afternoon I headed back for the dorm. I always checked my mail at the front desk before heading to my room and that afternoon was no exception. This time there was an unassuming envelope in my mailbox. It was a business letter and one that I didn't care to see—probably another bill. Upon opening it, my heart jumped. In the envelope there was a receipt for three hundred dollars that had been placed on my school bill. The very day I had prayed for help, it was there. God had come through and I couldn't believe it. I went back to my room and fell on my knees and wept. Today, I can't tell you how many times I have thought back to that experience and received a fresh inspiration that God *is* true to His word.

The fear I experienced in Mr. Show's office was now a distant memory—joy filled my heart.

I tried to find out who paid my school bill. There was no one I knew that would contribute this amount to a needy theology student. My parents were poor, so I was certain they did not send the money. Finally, someone told me that there had been a scholarship set aside for "worthy" ministerial students and they had decided to give the money to me.

The next semester began with a fresh sense of God's presence. I would still need money to go to school, and I was not certain where I would get it. One day, to my surprise, another three hundred dollars came in the mail. It was from my fiancée's father. My future father-in-law was very careful with his money so this gift was also unexpected. At the end of that summer, when I graduated, I did not owe any more than when I had begun the year, and I didn't borrow any either. What a blessing! A year later, after Jeanette and I were married, we received another unexpected gift of three hundred dollars, and then her two years of education were paid for while I went to the seminary. I had given God one hundred dollars in tithe, and He gifted us with five thousand dollars. I'd say that was a better return on my investment than Wall Street.

These events happened many years ago, but we have continued to trust God. We have learned that it is not *our* faithfulness that brings rewards but God's grace and His faithfulness that matters. We're now newly retired but rather than being in debt, our cars and modest home are paid for. Even more, God has passed on through us to our children a legacy of His faithfulness. They have experimented with Him, too, and He has been faithful to them. You can also experience God's faithfulness in your life. Trust Him and He will not fail you.

So, that's my story. From this experience and from my study of the Bible, my concept about God, tithe, and offerings has changed.

Let's now unpack the Malachi passage and find out what God

is telling us. Most likely, you have heard that passage read many times, but I want us to find out what God is telling us today.

God invites us to "test" Him

Nowhere else in Scripture do you find an admonition to test God, yet in this passage that is exactly what God invites us to do. If He fails to respond, He puts Himself at risk. In a day when faith is difficult, God says, "Try Me. See if I will not bless you." He challenges us to base our faith on the evidence of His faithfulness. In Malachi's time, Israel had not tested God and, as a result, they suffered the consequences. Things were not going well financially for God's people. Their crops were failing and animals were dying. They were wondering why they were having such hard times, and God showed them the reason for their problem—by withholding their tithes and offerings, they had shut down the storehouse. This passage tells us that if we faithfully return tithes and offerings, the windows of heaven will open. So, there we have it—test God and He will respond with a blessing.

God is real and you can count on Him

In spite of our technological advances and ability to view the mystery of the tiniest particles or largest star, God often seems intangible. We think that if God would only appear to us in some tangible way, we would trust Him more. But that is exactly what happens when we return the tithe and give offerings—God comes to us in a tangible way. We experience His faithfulness. Even now as I tell my story, God comes alive to me again. For me, tithing has been an avenue to growth and you, too, can experience that growth. My experience has helped me to know that I can count on Him.

God is a "Friend with benefits"

The idea that God will bless us if we are faithful to Him may seem strange to some. Yet, that is exactly what Malachi tells us. And God is not limited in His blessing. The psalmist tells us that He owns "the cattle on a thousand hills." The world is His. He does not need our sacrifices but He accepts our praises (Psalm 50:8–14, ESV). James reminds us that God has designed and bestowed on us every good gift (James 1:17). Think about it—God designs His gifts and then bestows them. That's God's promise to each of us.

Jesus talked about giving and blessings. He tells us, "Give, and it will be given to you. Good measure, pressed down, shaken together, running over" (Luke 6:38, ESV). He also reminds us that if we sow sparingly, we will reap sparingly. The disciples were not sure about the idea of giving, so they asked Jesus, "What are we going to get if we give up everything for You?" And Jesus replied, "[You will] receive a hundredfold now in this time, houses and brothers and sisters and mothers and children and lands, with persecutions, and in the age to come eternal life" (Mark 10:29, 30, ESV). What did Jesus mean by this? I believe He's telling us that we would experience blessings, even in this world. These blessings might be new brothers and sisters in Christ or even come in the form of houses or land. All of God's blessings are not only reserved for the future—many we can experience right now. I once knew a man who was wealthy. He made no profession of faith, but returned tithe because he said God always blessed him. In the act of giving, we discover the benefits of a connection with God. Faithful tithers such as J. C. Penney and John D. Rockefeller were blessed financially and gave large amounts of money to their churches and charities.

The benefit of protection

Malachi tells us of one more blessing. God promised His people that their crops would not fail and their livestock would be healthy. Many of us may not have crops or livestock, but God can still give us the benefit of protection. Just the other day, I was talking with a former high school classmate about this topic and mentioned how often the cars had lasted longer than expected. That's a blessing from God.

It may not seem logical to return tithe and live on only nine-tenths of our income, but God makes it work. It could be that God opens doors for employment we did not expect, or when we get a job that pays more. Or there are times when we receive funds we did not expect. I remember when our income was rather short for the month. We thought we would have to dip into our savings to survive. That very month, someone who owed us money returned it. We had actually assumed that the money would never be returned to us, but it was returned the very month we needed it. So, instead of having to borrow from our savings, we actually added to it. Sometimes it's hard to explain these blessings, but I know who makes them happen. God protects us in ways we do not even anticipate.

The struggle and the test

I told you about the struggle I experienced with the one hundred dollars of tithe I needed to return to God. In a way, these struggles are a test. You may have faced such a test. James writes these encouraging words about tests and struggles: "When all kinds of trials and temptations crowd into your lives my brothers, don't resent them as intruders, but welcome them as friends! Realise that they come to test your faith and to produce in you the quality of endurance. But let the process go on . . . and you will find you have become men of mature character with the right sort of independence" (James 1:2–4, Phillips). Abraham went through many struggles waiting for the birth of the promised son, but he and Sarah experienced the fulfillment of God's promise. Joseph was exiled to Egypt and eventually unjustly placed in a dungeon, but God used his terrible trial to prepare him for leadership in Egypt. Moses tried to help God by killing an abusive Egyptian guard. But when Moses trusted God, he was able to lead the Israelites from slavery to freedom. We all experience struggles and testing, and those experiences can strengthen the bonds between God and us.

Beyond the tithe

For many years, when I read Malachi, I limited its implications to tithe. But God said Israel had robbed Him in tithes *and* offerings. Does the same invitation to be faithful in offerings come to us today? Yes. In many cases, local churches or missions cannot survive without our offerings as well as tithes. Offerings are necessary for churches to pay the light bill, to help maintain a school, or build a church. Can we afford to give offerings as well as tithes? It has been estimated that the Israelites gave around 25 percent of their income to God. Granted, with the tax system in the North American territory, if we gave that amount to the church and paid the taxes, for most of us it would be rather difficult. But, lest we think we may become poverty stricken, our gifts often radically reduce our tax liability. I have discovered that if I give off the top in offerings (just like I do in tithe), somehow I don't seem to miss the amount given. Somehow God blesses us either financially or in some other way. On the other hand, I have found that investing in the stock market may not be as lucrative as I hoped. Some time ago, we invested in a stock that I thought was absolutely going to soar. After a few days, it more than doubled and we were elated. But predictions said it would more than double again in just a few days. So I left my dollars on the table, believing in the speculation of greater returns. Did that happen? No! Much to my chagrin, the investment lost all its value and the stock was worth zero in a few short months. Of course, there are success stories of those who have made better choices in more secure companies, but over the years, I've learned that investing with God brings better returns than the stock market, or any other investment, for that matter. Those returns are like treasures in heaven. It's like buying your cake and eating it too. So, God invites us to test Him, not only in tithes but also in offerings. He is the same today, yesterday, and forever. King David encouraged us with these words (and he ought to know), "If I go up to heaven, you are there; if I go down to the grave, you are there. If I ride the wings of the morning, if I dwell by the farthest oceans, even there your hand will guide me, and your strength will support me" (Psalm 139:8–10, NLT). That is a far better promise than the dividends on Wall Street.

Conclusion

What has been your experience? Perhaps your journey has been similar to mine. At some points, it seemed to you that it would be impossible to be faithful to God. But, ultimately, you found out that God would not fail you. That's the way God is—He is faithful to us, even at times when we are not faithful.

Some of you may be afraid to trust God. It just does not seem like all of your needs will be met if you return a faithful tithe and offering to God. My testimony to you is that God will not fail you. Trust Him. I trust Him and God has never failed me.

Think of this—if we trust God with our salvation—our eternal life—surely we can trust that He will care for our daily needs. In fact, trusting God with our daily needs helps us believe more completely that He can get us ready and keep us ready for heaven. God is faithful, and He will never forget us.

Multiplying and Unifying the Church Through Stewardship

G. Tom Carter

God created and blessed Adam and Eve and, at the same time, gave them privileges and responsibilities. The Bible states that "God blessed them, and God said to them, 'Be fruitful and multiply; fill the earth and subdue it; have dominion over the fish of the sea, over the birds of the air, and over every living thing that moves on the earth' " (Genesis 1:28, NKJV).

In this verse we read that Adam and Eve were to "have dominion." The expression "dominion" does not mean exploitation of the natural world, but rather sharing with God responsibility for the earth. After all, Adam and Eve were created in the image of God and they were capable of distinguishing between exploitation and stewardship. In fact, the *Andrews Study Bible,* commenting on Genesis 1:28, identifies stewardship by which creation would be unified, as well as, multiplied. Stewardship means that human beings are privileged, but with that privilege comes responsibility. As God's stewards, we are not owners of

God's earth. He is the Owner of all (Psalm 24:1, 2) and the Source of the power to get wealth (Deuteronomy 8:18).

God's multiplication principle

We are the product of multiplication. One source states that "More than 100 trillion cells make up the human body. Most of these cells contain all the genes and other information needed to 'build' a human being."[1] Starting from just one cell at conception, the cells multiply rapidly. We are told that, "The great rate of growth of the fetus compared with that of the child is largely due to the fact that cells are still multiplying. The proportion of cells undergoing mitosis (the ordinary process of cell multiplication by splitting) in any tissue becomes progressively less as the fetus gets older."[2] We understand why the psalmist states, "I will praise You, for I am fearfully and wonderfully made. . . . Your eyes saw my substance, being yet unformed" (Psalm 139:14, 16, NKJV).

God's promise to Abraham was, "I will bless you, and multiplying I will multiply your descendants as the stars of heaven" (Genesis 22:17, NKJV). Christ specifically applies this to spiritual children, "If you were Abraham's children, you would do the works of Abraham" (John 8:39, NKJV). And Paul verified the spiritual application when he said, "Just as Abraham 'believed God, and it was accounted to him for righteousness.' Therefore know that only those who are of faith are sons of Abraham" (Galatians 3:6, 7, NKJV). The Bible points to a partial fulfillment of the multiplication of Abraham's spiritual descendants with these words: "And walking in the fear of the Lord and in the comfort of the Holy Spirit, they were multiplied" (Acts 9:31, NKJV).

Stewardship and the multiplication process

Remember the New Testament story of the boy with the five barley loaves and two fish? The boy gives Jesus his lunch. Jesus multiplies that lunch and feeds some fifteen to twenty thousand people. It's interesting that this miracle story is the only one recorded in every one of the four Gospels. Christ could have performed the miracle without the young boy giving his lunch. But as always, Christ asks us to give something of ourselves so He can multiply it both for our good and the good of others. Remember the story of the widow of Zarephath and Elijah? She was asked to give her last bit of food and make a small cake of bread for Elijah before she baked something for her boy and herself (1 Kings 17:9–16).

And then there is the story of Elisha and the widow whose sons were about to be taken into slavery by her creditors. Elisha told her to ask all her neighbors for empty jars. In fact, Elisha told her not to ask for just a few jars, but all the jars she could collect. This is a mother who had no oil at all. She did as she was told and all of the jars were miraculously filled with oil. The oil stopped flowing after she no longer had any empty jars (2 Kings 4:1–7). This story of faith reminds us of Jesus' words, "Give, and it will be given you. A good measure, pressed down, shaken together and running over, will be poured into your lap" (Luke 6:38, NIV).

Stewardship is more than material possessions, food, or money. Peter and John demonstrated this principle in the story of the beggar who had physical handicaps from birth. The man was begging for money, but the apostles had no money to give him. Instead, Peter told him, "Silver or gold I do not have, but what I do have I give you." What Peter gave was more, much more—he gave the man the ability to walk again (Acts 3:1–10, NIV). At the same time, we should not think that God does not care what we do with our material assets. One writer tells us that, "Two-thirds of Jesus' parables deal with money and material possessions or our attitude towards them. There are well over two thousand Biblical references that deal with this topic, while there are only about five hundred verses on prayer and fewer than five hundred on faith. Obviously, God thinks Knowledge [and Stewardship] about money is very important."[3] Just think, two-thirds of the parables deal with material possessions.

Let me tell you about a couple who had the biblical understanding of stewardship. Frank and Evelyn Moran had spent their years of service in the educational field. When I met them, he taught at Loma Linda University. He had inherited a fifty-five-acre farm from his parents and instead of giving the usual 10 percent to the Lord, they had decided to give *90* percent and keep the 10 percent. The land was put in trust with the Texas Conference of Seventh-day Adventists. At the time of the gift, the land was worth about fifty-five thousand dollars. Eventually, plans were made to build the Dallas/Fort Worth International Airport near the property. The property was sold and I had the privilege of receiving, on behalf of the conference, a check for $1,244,113.53. The church was blessed and also the Morans—even though what they kept was only 10 percent of the gift they received from his parents—they received a significant amount from the sale of the land.[4]

God's multiplication process continues after death

Death is a reality that we all face. Yet, God does not forget His children who die. The Bible tells us that John the revelator heard these words: "Then I heard a voice from heaven say, 'Write this: Blessed are the dead who die in the Lord from now on.' 'Yes,' says the Spirit, 'they will rest from their labor, for their deeds will follow them' " (Revelation 14:13, NIV). I believe from Bible principles that these works will not only follow but that they multiply. Ellen G. White writes these encouraging words:

> When a man dies, his influence does not die
> with him; but it lives on, reproducing itself. The
> influence of the man who was good and pure and
> holy lives on after his death, like the glow of the
> descending sun, casting its glories athwart the

heavens, lighting up the mountain peaks long after the sun has sunk behind the hill. So will the works of the pure and the holy and the good reflect their light when they no longer live to speak and act themselves. Their works, their words, their example will forever live. "The righteous shall be in everlasting remembrance."[5]

A few years ago, my wife, Janette, and I were pleased that Medal of Honor recipient Desmond T. Doss and his wife, Francis, would be staying with us. They attended our church for a special church service. Members and visitors were inspired by the thrilling story of how God had enabled Desmond to save seventy-five men in a terrible battle during World War II. As I listened to Desmond Doss, I realized how much God had multiplied his life because he was willing to give so much for God and others. When he died, he arranged that his humble estate would bless his family and the Lord's work. The rights to his life story were given to the church, now having been televised to millions.[6]

For the Christian steward, making plans so that both family needs and the Lord's work are remembered brings peace. I was blessed to know Denton E. Rebok and his wife, Marie. They wanted to make sure the Lord was generously remembered in their future plans. So they both made two substantial gifts in a form that would give them income during their lifetime, and at their deaths, the remainder would be gifted to the church. Denton Rebok wrote before his death, "Since making the arrangements . . . my wife and I can testify that we have experienced great relief and peace now fills our hearts."[7] Their works are still being multiplied.

Christian stewardship unifies

Christ earnestly prayed for unity among His followers. John records Jesus praying "that they all may be one, as You,

Father, are in Me, and I in You; that they also may be one in Us, that the world may believe that You sent Me" (John 17:21, NKJV). Unity is dependent on being one with the Father and Son. This is accomplished when we put self aside and willingly give in the same spirit as Christ gave His life for us. Christian stewardship, I believe, can be defined as making Jesus the Lord and Savior in all that we have and do. Paul defined stewardship and serving Christ as interchangeable. He writes, "Let a man so consider us, as servants of Christ and stewards of the mysteries of God. Moreover it is required in stewards that one be found faithful" (1 Corinthians 4:1, 2, NKJV).

Remember our reference to the multiplication of cells? Despite the fact that we multiply from one cell to over one hundred trillion, the outcome is one body. Every cell somehow is mysteriously connected and must work together. We understand little of how this is accomplished. Albert Claude, a biologist, said, "Man, like other organisms, is so perfectly coordinated that he may easily forget . . . that he is a colony of cells in action."[8] The church is composed of many members all working together under one Head, Jesus Christ (1 Corinthians 12). We are to use our time, talents, and material blessings both to multiply and unify the body.

Using stewardship to multiply and unify the local church

The Letter to the Ephesians gives a beautiful picture of the worldwide, as well as local, church. Paul writes, "Instead, we will speak the truth in love, growing in every way more and more like Christ, who is the head of his body, the church. *He makes the whole body fit together perfectly. As each part does its own special work, it helps the other parts grow, so that the whole body is healthy and growing and full of love*" (Ephesians 4:15, 16, NLT; emphasis supplied). We are not to give up if our church does not resemble this ideal model in every aspect. Even the apostolic church, while at times seeming to fulfill the model, experienced times of stagnation and disunity. It is so important that we move closer to the biblical model of the church. Ellen White comments:

> There are lay members who are fitted to bear responsibilities, and who would do so if there were some one with patience, kindness, and forbearance, who would teach them how to work. Ministers should show a real earnestness in helping such persons to succeed, and should put forth persevering effort to develop talent. The inexperienced are in need of wise generals who by prayer and personal effort will encourage and help them to become perfect in Christ Jesus. This is the work which every gospel minister should endeavor to do.[9]

In addition to helping each member find where he or she can work most effectively, financial stewardship must be fostered. We can't dedicate our lives without dedicating our pocketbooks, and we can't dedicate our pocketbooks without dedicating our lives. The two go together. God tells us, "They shall not appear before the LORD empty-handed. Every man shall give as he is able, according to the blessing of the LORD your God which He has given you" (Deuteronomy 16:16, 17, NKJV). We need to give financially and materially "according to the blessing of the Lord," as the Bible tells us.

How do we do it?

How do we remind ourselves what stewardship is about? How do we become faithful stewards? There are specific ways that we can become the stewards God wants us to be.

We need to remind ourselves that stewardship begins and ends with love. All of our church activities and functions must reflect this love. Love is not just speaking the right words. Love is reflected in our actions. The Bible tells us that "God so loved the world, that he gave his only begotten Son" (John 3:16, KJV). God's love is costly. It is by beholding this love on the cross that we are willing to give. Christ said, "Freely you have received, freely give" (Matthew 10:8, NKJV).

Secondly, just as our bodies are made up of trillions of cells, these cells must function together in order to make the body complete. Our churches are made up of individuals, but we need to function as a body. There must be a community of believers. Ellen White emphasizes these needs for community:

> The Lord in His wisdom has arranged that by means of the close relationship that should be maintained by all believers, Christian shall be united to Christian, and church to church. . . .
>
> As all the different members of the human system unite to form the entire body, and each performs its office in obedience to the intelligence that governs the whole, so the members of the church of Christ should be united in one symmetrical body, subject to the sanctified intelligence of the whole.[10]

Thirdly, we need to remind ourselves of the challenging words Jesus spoke to His followers. Jesus said, "But you shall receive power when the Holy Spirit has come upon you; and you shall be witnesses to Me in Jerusalem, and in all Judea and Samaria, and to the end of the earth" (Acts 1:8, NKJV). What a challenge for this little group of believers to witness to the whole world. Our job is to break this down for every member so they can be challenged to fulfill their individual role locally, as well as their responsibility to the worldwide church.

Fourthly, the Word of God tells us to have our priorities straight. Jesus says, "But seek first the kingdom of God and His righteousness, and all these things shall be added to you" (Matthew 6:33, NKJV). Jesus is not telling us to ignore our personal or family needs. He *does* tell us to first seek God's kingdom and righteousness. When we first seek God's kingdom and righteousness, we are exercising the faith Jesus gives us. For we are told that "without faith it is impossible to please Him" (Hebrews 11:6, NKJV).

Finally, God calls for commitment. Not commitment to just anything, but commitment to God's eternal values. This commitment is not something we make once in our lives, rather it is a daily personal commitment to God.

Conclusion

Christian stewardship involves the total person. We need to keep it fresh in our lives by Bible study, prayer, and meditation on God's Word. We need to focus on Christ's ministry for us. If we, as church members, live such lives, we will achieve God's model for the church. The well-known preacher Henry Ward Beecher stated,

> Consecration is not wrapping one's self in a holy web in the sanctuary and then coming forth after prayer and twilight meditation and saying, "There I am consecrated." Consecration is going out into the world, where God Almighty is, and using every power for His glory. It is taking all advantages as trust funds—as confidential debts owed to God. It is simply dedicating one's life in its whole flow, to God's service.[11]

Faithful stewards are individuals who have been transformed by the Holy Spirit.

Ellen White put it this way:

> The work of transformation from unholiness to holiness is a continuous one. Day by day God labors for man's sanctification, and man is to

co-operate with Him, putting forth persevering efforts in the cultivation of right habits. He is to add grace to grace; and *as he thus works on the plan of addition, God works for him on the plan of multiplication.*[12]

Just as God made Adam and Eve stewards of His creation, He makes us stewards of His gifts to us, ushering us into the joy of faithful stewardship. All of us can experience the "exceedingly abundant" blessings it brings.

Endnotes

1. "Human Cells 101," http://www.tititudorancea.org/z/human_cells_101.htm (accessed January 14, 2013).

2. "Human Development," s.v. *Encyclopedia Britannica,* Online Library Edition, July 20, 2012.

3. G. Edward Reid, ed., *Faith and Finance: Financial Planning With a Faith Factor* (Silver Spring, Md.: Stewardship Department, North American Division of Seventh-day Adventists, 2009), 7, 8.

4. Frank Moran, "The Story of the Irving Property in Texas," *The Southwestern Union Record* (73), May 11, 1974, 11.

5. Ellen G. White, *Testimonies to Ministers and Gospel Workers* (Mountain View, Calif.: Pacific Press® Publishing Association, 1962), 429.

6. G. Tom Carter, "Passing on Values, not Just Material Assets," *Southern Tidings* (104:8), August 2012, 4–7.

7. Denton E. Rebok, "The Only Way to Beat Inflation," *Adventist Review,* December 27, 1979.

8. Allen R. Glanville, *All of Science* (Elanora Heights, NSW, Australia: Millennium House, 2010), 274.

9. Ellen G. White, *The Review and Herald,* June 27, 1912.

10. Ellen G. White, *Counsels for the Church* (Nampa, Idaho: Pacific Press®, 1991), 247.

11. Henry Ward Beecher, quoted in Transformation Garden Web site, www.wfia-fm.com/devotionals/11654019/page2/print (accessed July 29, 2011).

12. Ellen G. White, *The Acts of the Apostles* (Mountain View, Calif.: Pacific Press®, 1911), 532; emphasis supplied.

Called to Share

Gerry Christman

Nabal, a sheep owner, was more than wealthy—he was super rich. He owned three thousand sheep and one thousand goats. In his day, that made him very rich.

Sheep need shearing once a year—usually in the spring. Can you imagine shearing thousands of animals without electric clippers? Sheep, fortunately, become still and cannot wiggle when they are on their backs with all four feet in the air. It takes great skill for shearers to flip sheep onto their backs, but once done, shearers can cut wool from passive sheep. Shearing is a huge job, but Nabal, of course, had plenty of hired workers to help get it done.

Once the sheep were shorn, *everyone* rejoiced. This time of rejoicing was more than just payday for the workers. It was party time for all—a time to celebrate. The festivities included family, friends, and servants; everyone living in close proximity was invited—foreigners, strangers, and the poor. After the *shearing* came the *sharing*.

Another example of biblical hospitality comes from the time of Nehemiah. What did Nehemiah instruct his people to do?

"Then he said to them, 'Go your way, eat the fat, drink the sweet, and send portions to those for whom nothing is prepared.' . . . And all the people went their way to eat and drink, to send portions and rejoice greatly" (Nehemiah 8:10–12).[1] Sharing, giving away food and drink, was a top priority. Fun times were to extend beyond family and friends. It was an opportunity to share God's blessings.

But, let's go back to the time of Nabal—that was also the time of David. David and his men looked in anticipation to the festivities soon to take place at Nabal's Ranch. David, as you remember, had been hiding in nearby caves, trying to elude jealous King Saul. David and his men had protected Nabal's shepherds and sheep from bandits and wild animals— but David was not seeking compensation from Nabal.

David and his men were living near Nabal's place. According to custom, they should have been included at Nabal's party, but the invitation never came. So what did David do? The Bible tells us that

> David sent ten young men; and David said to the young men, "Go up to Carmel, go to Nabal, and greet him in my name. And thus you shall say to him who lives in prosperity: 'Peace be to you, peace to your house, and peace to all that you have! Now I have heard that you have shearers. Your shepherds were with us, and we did not hurt them, nor was there anything missing from them all the while they were in Carmel. Ask your young men, and they will tell you. Therefore let my young men find favor in your eyes, for we come on a feast day. Please give whatever comes to your hand to your servants and to your son David' " (1 Samuel 25:5–8).

Does it not seem brash for David's men to invite themselves

to Nabal's party? Not at all. David was not a beggar—he was simply following a code of conduct. God had given specific instructions regarding who was to come to such social events. Scripture states, "You shall rejoice in your feast, you and your son and your daughter, your male servant and your female servant and the Levite, the stranger and the fatherless and the widow, who are within your gates" (Deuteronomy 16:14).

God instructs us to invite individuals we might leave off our list. He especially wants us to remember the destitute, lonely, foreigners—those who are often forgotten.

So how does Nabal react to the request from David's men? We are told in 1 Samuel, "So when David's young men came, they spoke to Nabal according to all these words in the name of David, and waited" (25:9). Picture the scene. David's ten men made their modest request and waited. Nabal was quiet— an awkward silence. Instead, Nabal humiliated them by making them wait. It's as if Nabal pondered whether David and his men were worthy or not. Nabal should have felt ashamed that these men had to come and ask. He should have apologized for not having already invited them to his feast. But Nabal was selfish—and foolish.

Finally, Nabal answered them, but notice how: " 'Who is David, and who is the son of Jesse? There are many servants nowadays who break away each one from his master. Shall I then take my bread and my water and my meat that I have killed for my shearers, and give it to men when I do not know where they are from?' " (verses 10, 11).

Nabal responded rhetorically; his questions didn't seek information; they were meant to insult. He demeaned David by asking, "Who is David?" David, of course, was a national hero, and Nabal knew who David was. He continued his condescending response by asking, "Who is the son of Jesse?" Nabal implied that David was a "nobody," that he was irrelevant. Nabal dismissed David as if he were a worthless hooligan. But he was not finished with his meanness. "Shall

I then take my bread and my water and my meat that I have killed for my shearers, and give it to men when I do not know where they are from?" (verse 11).

Nabal demonstrated a distorted worldview. He believed the things under his roof were his and his alone. "*My* bread, *my* water, *my* shearers"—that was his focus. He allowed greed to condition his mind. Greed closed Nabal's eyes where he no longer saw God as the Source of every good thing.

Nabal should have known better. He was a descendant of Caleb—a great man of faith. Nabal knew his duty and responsibility. He knew God had designed that those with abundance should supply those who lacked; that we are our brother's keeper. Nabal had a God-given obligation to keep an eye out for strangers within his gates, but Nabal closed his eyes, and so the Bible calls him a fool.

Many years later, Jesus tells us, "When you give a feast, invite the poor, the maimed, the lame, the blind. And you will be blessed, because they cannot repay you; for you shall be repaid at the resurrection of the just" (Luke 14:13, 14). Helping those in need is not just a good idea. It's actually a mandate from Jesus.

Is there an individual or a family that has been excluded from your circle? You and I are to share what God has given us with these individuals. What about our church? Do we share our blessings with the church? That's the question Jesus is asking us.

Prince William of Great Britain was born into a royal and rich family. In spite of his royalty and wealth, he demonstrated concern for the homeless. Before his marriage in 2011, he reportedly spent a night sleeping in freezing weather on a London street. He wanted to experience the plight of the poor.[2] On another occasion, he attended an event for a homelessness charity. This is where he met Shozna. Shozna suffered a stroke as a teenager. The right side of her body was paralyzed. A series of tragedies led her to become homeless at eighteen.

Prince William, at the time of the wedding, remembered Shozna and sent her an invitation to his wedding. Shozna underwent a complete makeover before she attended Prince William and Kate Middleton's wedding. Shozna said she "felt beautiful" sitting among royalty at Westminster Abbey.[3]

When it's time to celebrate, let's not remember just family and friends. God wants us to intentionally include the poor, afflicted, and lonely. Just how important it is to care for the needy is illustrated by the cities of Sodom and Gomorrah. Those cities are known for their wickedness. Why did God destroy Sodom? The Bible states, " 'Now this was the sin of your sister Sodom: She and her daughters were arrogant, overfed and unconcerned; they did not help the poor and needy' " (Ezekiel 16:49, NIV). God rained fire upon Sodom—not just because of her sexual and other perversions, but because they did not extend their hands to those in need.

Three kinds of people

John Maxwell writes that there are three kinds of people: Takers, Traders, and Investors.[4] Everyone knows who the takers are. They are the Nabals in society. They take more than they give. They wait for others to give so that they can enjoy the benefits. They love to make "withdrawals" while they expect others to make "deposits." A community full of takers is devastating; but a church full of takers is worse. Takers ignore God's expressed commands to share God's blessings.

The second group is traders. Traders are also foolish. They give in order to receive. Traders are busy looking for their own set of friends. They may be generous with their friends, but they also keep a close eye on what they receive in return. Traders prefer being Takers—but they recognize it is socially unacceptable. Nabal was a taker, but by necessity he was also a trader.

Then there are investors. Investors are the wise stewards in God's kingdom. Investors actively look for ways to help.

They look for strangers in church so that they can be friendly to them. They go out of their way to help those who are in need. Their eyes are quick to notice what needs to be done and they do it. They give freely to support the church's ministries. Investors for God are focused on God's kingdom—not on themselves. They give without a thought of receiving anything in return. They know that it is more blessed to give than to receive.

In the New Testament, the church at Macedonia was full of investors. They were financially poor, but nevertheless they were investors. Notice what they did:

> Moreover, brethren, we make known to you the grace of God bestowed on the churches of Macedonia: that in a great trial of affliction the abundance of their joy and *their deep poverty abounded in the riches of their liberality*. For I bear witness that according to their ability, yes, and beyond their ability, they were freely willing, imploring us with much urgency that we would receive the gift and the fellowship of the ministering to the saints. And not only as we had hoped, but they first gave themselves to the Lord, and then to us by the will of God (2 Corinthians 8:1–5; emphasis supplied).

These church members were poor—yet they begged for the honor of sharing. They considered giving to be a privilege—not a burden or an obligation. How did this happen? Verse 5 answers this question. They *first* gave themselves to the Lord, and *then* they opened up their hearts and wallets. They gave above and beyond because they had first given their lives to God.

What about us?

How is it with us? Are we takers, traders, or investors? How would you classify yourself? Do we like to take, trade, or are we willing investors?

Many years ago I taught at a school. A fellowship meal was planned for the faculty, and everyone was asked to bring food. The plan was to celebrate the Lord's Supper after enjoying a meal together. I envisioned tables bountifully laden with tasty homemade dishes—plenty of food for all. It was disappointing to see most of the families arriving with small plates of food. Each family was hoping, of course, that others would bring generous amounts of food. The meal was headed for disaster because too many demonstrated "taker" traits. The school's food service director, fortunately, came to our rescue by pulling large cans of food from the cafeteria pantry.

Generosity is an attribute that is seen not only in the actions of the wealthy. The poor, in fact, are often proportionately more generous. Our family served as missionaries in a poor region of Brazil. Frequently, needy children came to our house asking for bread. My wife, one day, gave a large slice of homemade bread to a boy who had come to our door. The boy, however, did not immediately start eating the bread. A group of friends were waiting for him, and once he left our house, they soon formed a circle around him. He then tore off a piece for everyone before he ate the last bite. The joy of sharing was more important than filling his own stomach. His act of sharing made him an investor in others.

Our response

So how do we react when others don't give the way we think they should? How do we respond when we personally suffer as a result of exclusiveness and selfishness? Do we harbor resentment and anger?

The Bible tells us that David was furious when his men returned and told him what Nabal had said about him. David quickly decided to teach Nabal an unforgettable lesson: he planned to kill Nabal. This story, fortunately, did not end with murder because Abigail, Nabal's peacemaker wife, sprang into action. Nabal deserved judgment, but David was not the one to render it. We can never make things right by doing wrong. As the prophet Amos tell us, "For I know your manifold transgressions and your mighty sins: afflicting the just and taking bribes; diverting the poor from justice at the gate. Therefore the prudent keep silent at that time, for it is an evil time" (Amos 5:12, 13). Even when injustice is done to us, it is best to depend on God to make things right. God, in His own way and time, will make things right.

Jesus tells us that God looks at our actions. Listen to the words of Jesus:

> "Then the King will say to those on His right hand, 'Come, you blessed of My Father, inherit the kingdom prepared for you from the foundation of the world: for I was hungry and you gave Me food; I was thirsty and you gave Me drink; I was a stranger and you took Me in; I was naked and you clothed Me; I was sick and you visited Me; I was in prison and you came to Me.' . . . And the King will answer and say to them, 'Assuredly, I say to you, inasmuch as you did it to one of the least of these My brethren, you did it to Me' " (Matthew 25:34–40).

How do we treat others? How do we treat the needy? What kind of stewards are we? These are questions we need to continually ask ourselves.

My mother-in-law was constantly on the alert for people in need. She often invited to her home people who needed help or encouragement. Thanksgiving and Christmas for her were not just about family—they were opportunities to intentionally include the lonely. My job was to go and pick up anyone who did not have transportation. Martha, as I will call her, did not have a car, so I drove across town to pick her up.

She lived alone in a run-down motel room and was always thrilled to be included. Martha, one year, brought a gift; it was a large framed picture of her. I admit that sooner or later I would have tucked that large photo out of sight, but this is not what my mother-in-law did. She hung it in a prominent place in the hallway where it remained for years. I passed Martha's picture in the hallway countless times, and seeing her picture was a subtle reminder that *everybody* is important. My mother-in-law's actions were a wonderful gift to her children and grandchildren. They learned that people like Martha are to be at the top of our invitation list. When we help others, we really help ourselves. Stewardship means we are faithful to God and share God's blessings with others. When we are generous with others, we are being generous with Jesus. Winston Churchill said, "We make a living by what we get, but we make a life by what we give."[5]

Conclusion

Until the Lord Jesus Christ returns, there will be Takers, Traders, and Investors. The followers of Jesus Christ are called to share, just as Jesus shared. He shared His life so that we may live eternally. We share not because we have to, but because, as followers of Jesus, we are faithful stewards who willingly share God's blessings.

Endnotes

1. All Bible texts, unless otherwise indicated, are taken from New King James Version.

2. www.dailymail.co.uk/news/article-1237773/Prince-William-sleeps-rough-streets-London-experience-life-homeless.html.

3. http://londonmuslims.blogspot.com/2011/04/shozna-homeless-muslim-royal-wedding.html, www.dailymail.co.uk/news/article-1377756/Royal-Wedding-Homeless-girl-Shozna-20-wowed-Prince-William-invited.html

4. John C. Maxwell, "The Boomerang Principle" in *Winning With People Workbook* (Nashville, Tenn.: Nelson Impact, 2004), 197.

5. http://thinkexist.com/quotation/we_make_a_living_by_what_we_get -but_we_make_a/14355.html.

Those Mighty Mites

Ernest Dobkins

As a boy growing up in the late 1940s, I frequented the local movie house. Often the movie theater had a double feature and also what was called "short subjects," between the feature films. Occasionally, they would show a cartoon with the character of "Mighty Mouse." Mighty Mouse was a takeoff on "Superman," and kids loved to see it. Just like Superman, Mighty Mouse could leap tall buildings, stop trains, and speed faster than a bullet. In my mind as a child, he was "Super Mouse." I thought of this small wonder mouse when I read Mark 12:41–44:

> Now Jesus sat opposite the treasury and saw
> how the people put money into the treasury. And
> many who were rich put in much. Then one poor
> widow came and threw in two mites, which make
> a quadrans. So He called His disciples to Himself
> and said to them, "Assuredly, I say to you that this
> poor widow has put in more than all those who have
> given to the treasury; for they all put in out of their
> abundance, but she out of her poverty put in all that

she had, her whole livelihood" (NKJV).

Those mites, according to the Bible, are the smallest
amount that one could give. They were physically small as
well, about the diameter of a pencil eraser. But the size of
the mite is not the point. The fact that Jesus places such high
value on these particular mites is the point. They become, in
my mind, on equal par with "Mighty Mouse."

Let's go back to the story Jesus told. The woman made her
way through the crowd. Her goal was to get into the temple
area called the Court of Women. It was the only place she
was allowed to mingle with men. I imagine her pressed by
the crowd, pushing toward the thirteen trumpet-shaped offering containers until she had clear access to one of them. I
believe she noticed some individuals with not just a handful
of coins, or two like herself, but bags full. She clutched her
mites more tightly. Finally, she dared to get close enough to
throw her two small coins into the container. The containers
rang with the sounds of coins of different sizes, weights, and
values, making music to the ears of the priests. No doubt
when the woman's coins were tossed into the offering funnel,
their sound was different from the sound of the more valuable coins. Her coins just did not sound important.

What was happening in the temple was big business. Pil-
grims came from many and distant countries eager to display their faithfulness with the money they saved for this
occasion. They brought all kinds of coins with them. There
were large gold coins, and they sounded important as they
descended into the containers. The silver denarius is about
the size of a dime, but it is said to be a day's pay for a Roman
soldier. There were all kinds of copper and brass coins. Because of the variety of coins, moneychangers were needed at
the temple.

We don't know the name or many other details of the
woman in Jesus' story. We do know that she was a widow

and that a widow's life was hard. If she were living today, she might be eligible for a pension, some government programs, or help with her food costs. But that was not the case in Jesus' day. She depended on the good graces of others. Sometimes a widow's family helped, but without that help, she often depended on begging or even selling her body to strangers.

Recently, I went shopping at a large mall with my wife and another woman. Better said, they were shopping; I was simply with them. When I am in the mall, I usually sit on a bench watching people. Apparently, that's what Jesus was doing at the temple—watching people. Mark tells us, "Now Jesus sat opposite the treasury and saw how people put money into the treasury. And many who were rich put in much" (Mark 12:41, NKJV). Jesus saw all kinds of people from various countries. However, He seemed to be focused on the coffers and the amounts going into them.

Imagine you are there with Jesus watching the people depositing their coins. All kinds of people are there—men, women, old, and young. Some of them are from Jerusalem, while others are from distant places. Some of those who have traveled for many days are overjoyed that they have made it to the temple. Their dream of visiting the temple is finally fulfilled.

Jesus focused on one person—not the best dressed or richest. He focused on a woman whose dress announces to all that she is poor—a widow, clutching two coins.

Coins are interesting objects—many of them have a rich history. Some have very little value while others are extremely valuable. Many coins have a value that is much greater than when they were originally put into circulation. I want to tell you about such a coin. Many consider it to be the most valuable coin.

According to Wikipedia, one of the most valuable coins is a 1933 double eagle gold coin, originally worth twenty dollars.[1] Double eagle coins were minted between 1850 and

1933. They were called double eagles because the largest coin minted before the California Gold Rush was a ten dollar gold piece with an eagle on one side and a standing liberty figure on the other.

Franklin D. Roosevelt, as newly elected president, had to face the devastating consequences of the Great Depression. He issued an executive order announcing that, with few exceptions, it was illegal to possess gold coins and bullion. This order applied even to the 1933 double eagle coins. The 1933 coins, 445,500 of them, were not put into circulation, but were to be melted. Two of the coins, however, survived the meltdown and were given to the Smithsonian Institute for display. Then, the unthinkable happened—more began to appear. Upon investigation by the U.S. Secret Service, it was determined that the U.S. Mint's chief cashier had stolen ten of them. Nine were recovered and the last one somehow became the possession of King Farouk of Egypt. In 1952, King Farouk was deposed, and his coin collection was sold at auction. The U.S. Government claimed the coin and demanded that it be returned to the United States, but that did not happen. Somehow, it came into the hands of a British coin dealer, Stephen Fenton, who, in 1996, brought it to the Waldorf Astoria Hotel in New York City to sell. Because it is illegal to own a 1933 double eagle gold piece, he was arrested and the coin was taken. He fought the charges against him, and finally the case was settled out of court. The settlement was an agreement to sell the coin at auction and the proceeds divided between the government and Fenton.

What happened to the coin? In 2002, Sotheby's auctioned it in New York to an anonymous buyer. The twenty-dollar gold coin was sold for $7.59 million. It is said to be the most valuable coin in the world.

Let's go back to Jesus, who watched the widow put in her coins. We are told that she "came and threw in two mites, which make a quadrans" (Mark 12:42, NKJV). Two small copper coins—that's it. You and I are surprised just as the disciples were surprised because these two coins had very little value. They were the smallest, cheapest, most worthless coins at that time. Just as few of us stop to pick up a penny today, it may be that few stopped to pick up mites then. They simply were not worth the effort.

But what did Jesus say about the widow and the coins? "He called His disciples to Himself and said to them, 'Assuredly, I say to you that this poor widow has put in more than all those who have given to the treasury' " (verse 43, NKJV).

The disciples did not question Jesus on how He came to that conclusion. Though surprised, they realized that the value of any gift is the value that Jesus places on it. Just as the price or value of a coin, rare or not, is the value placed on it by the one who ultimately pays the price or receives the benefit. Jesus' kingdom was the ultimate beneficiary of the woman's gift.

Ellen White gives a graphic description of what happened at the temple:

> At the beginning of His ministry, Christ had driven from the temple those who defiled it by their unholy traffic; and His stern and godlike demeanor had struck terror to the hearts of the scheming traders. At the close of His mission He came again to the temple, and found it still desecrated as before. The condition of things was even worse than before. The outer court of the temple was like a vast cattle yard. With the cries of the animals and the sharp chinking of coin was mingled the sound of angry altercation between traffickers, and among them were heard the voices of men in sacred office. The dignitaries of the temple were themselves engaged in buying and selling and the exchange of money. So

completely were they controlled by their greed of gain that in the sight of God they were no better than thieves.[2]

Jesus should have been seated in the temple, welcomed by the civic and religious leaders, instructing the nation in righteousness, which would have led to Israel's becoming all that the prophets had proclaimed. It was to be the nation thronged to by the multitudes because it would have been a land flowing with milk and honey. Indeed, it was to be the Promised Land for many people.

Jesus did not focus on the fact that the leaders did not accept Him. He focused on the widow and her motive, her desire to help, even in her state of obvious need. That's why He proclaimed that her coins had more value than all the others added together. Even though society seemed to be against her, even ignoring the laws to take care of widows, she contributed to the very institution that was working against her place in society.

What about today?

What about today? How many do you know who don't attend, don't support the church because of a local elder, preacher, local church leaders, or a member? They don't come, don't give, and don't seem to care anymore. The widow had every reason to avoid religion and its leaders. But I think she said to herself, "I must attend the services, I must do what I can, I will not cease worshiping my God. I will be faithful to God."

Did Jesus say above the crowd, "Woman, you, the one with the two mites, stop, stop. What are you doing, you only have two mites? Keep them, come here, we'll give you a few from our bag"? No, He was moved by her determination. He would not rob her of this moment for all the money in the world. In fact, if all the money in the world had been there, He would still have said, "She gave more than all of them."

Once more Ellen White gives us an insight to the widow that brings hope to all of us. "The Saviour called His disciples to Him, and bade them mark the widow's poverty. Then His words of commendation fell upon her ear: 'Of a truth I say unto you, that this poor widow hath cast in more than they all.' Tears of joy filled her eyes as she felt that her act was understood and appreciated."[3]

I had not realized that she heard the approval of Jesus. I had not realized that her act brought comfort to her own heart by hearing another's approval. But, is it not true that we all want to know that what we do to advance the kingdom of God, no matter how much or little is given, is appreciated by Him?

I don't care how much you put in the offering today, this month, this year. I don't care what the church treasurer thinks about yours or my offering pattern. It does not matter if the conference treasurer is happy or not about the tithe report that comes from this church. The One that we must please is Jesus. What value does He place on what you give? What value does He place on what I give? That's the all-important question. If Jesus were here today as the plate is being passed, whom would He point to and say, "That one there gave more than all the rest"? Who will be that one? Will you be the one? Will I be the one? Only Jesus knows.

The value of coins goes up and down, depending on what one is willing to pay and how the economy is at that moment. I understand that ten more of the double eagles turned up in the estate of a jeweler. How would you feel after paying $7.59 million for a coin because of its rarity, the most valuable coin in the world, only to find out later there were ten more? The newly discovered coins were promptly confiscated and, after court proceedings that ended in July 2011, they were determined to be the property of the United States government. They are being held in Fort Knox, Kentucky, until further determinations are made.[4] Though one cannot be sure of what the value of a coin may be in the future, we know what value Jesus places on the coin owner—no matter what the value of the coin is. Just think of how many people through the ages have been inspired to give because of the lady in our story. Has her story inspired you?

I have worked in trust administration for many years, and I could tell you numerous stories of widows, and other church members, giving their money to the appeals that come to them. Many of them run out of money. Many do not even have two mites left to give. They have given until they have no more to give. I have not met one who has been sorry. That's the kind of giving that Jesus saw when the widow gave her coins.

Who among us has what Jesus would consider the most valuable coins? Just as coin collectors look for rare or lost coins, Jesus continues to mystify us all when He looks into the heart, reads the mind, and knows the motivation of His followers. He points at them giving their offerings, and tells all heaven, "Look, that one over there. That one gave more than all."

This is what I would like you to remember. It does not matter what value others place on our love, sacrifice, or offerings to advance the kingdom. It only matters what value Jesus places on them.

Endnotes

1. http://en.wikipedia.org/wiki/1933_double_eagle (accessed February 3, 2013).

2. Ellen G. White, *The Desire of Ages* (Nampa, Idaho: Pacific Press®, 1940), 589.

3. Ibid., 615.

4. http://en.wikipedia.org/wiki/1933_double_eagle (accessed February 3, 2013).

Investing in Heaven

Daniel B. Martella

Some years ago there was a man who had it all—so it seemed. The only thing in life he wanted was more of everything. He wanted more money, so he took his inheritance and, through shrewd business dealings, turned it into a billion dollars. He wanted more fame, so he became a Hollywood director and producer. He wanted more pleasure, so he paid big money to fulfill every fantasy he imagined. He wanted more thrills, so he flew the fastest airplanes. He wanted more power, so, according to one source, he tried to buy the influence of two United States presidents. His life goal was to always seek more things of this world, but it seemed he never achieved his goals.

That man, Howard Hughes, at the end of his life was nothing more than an empty shell of a man. He was emaciated and colorless. His fingernails grew out in long corkscrews. His mouth was full of rotten black teeth and his arms were riddled with needle marks. The poor man was a billionaire junkie who went insane believing in the myth of more.[1]

The problem is that many people still believe in the myth—if we can just fall into wealth; if we move into that big house; if we only had fancy clothes; if we had luxury cars and could take expensive vacations to exotic places—life would be wonderful. Too many think that if these wishes were fulfilled, they would live happily ever after.

Then Jesus spoke

In the Sermon on the Mount, Jesus got one-on-one with a crowd who wanted more—they were not different from many of us. They liked the good life. They liked having wealth and showing it off. They liked racing around town in their sporty chariots. Many of them liked hosting lavish parties in their fancy homes. They enjoyed being noticed—they wanted others to notice even their religious lives. Every time they went to the synagogue and put an offering in the plate, they hoped others would notice what they gave. Some of them, when they prayed, stood on the street corners and made a big production of it. When they fasted, they put on their holy, haggard faces. One look at them and people would say, "Wow! They've got it all!" But listen to the words Jesus spoke to them:

> "Do not store up for yourselves treasures on earth, where moths and vermin destroy, and where thieves break in and steal. But store up for yourselves treasures in heaven, where moths and vermin do not destroy, and where thieves do not break in and steal. For where your treasure is, there your heart will be also" (Matthew 6:19–21, NIV).

But Jesus did not speak these words only to those gathered around Him on that day. Jesus speaks those words to each of us.

Earthly treasure

When Jesus talks about earthly treasure, He is not saying that it is a sin to be wealthy or that we need to get rid of all our possessions and take a vow of poverty. The Bible is filled with the stories of godly men and women who were wealthy; just think of Job, Abraham, Joseph, Daniel, Nicodemus, and Lydia—to name a few. At the same time, Jesus does not want us to make the acquisition of wealth the most important thing in our lives. And so, in the Sermon on the Mount, He is not talking about what you *own*—He's talking about *what* owns you. He's not talking about *what* we have—He's talking about *where* our treasure is.

I heard a story about four brothers who set a goal of doing some outstanding things. One day they came together to compare their accomplishments. The first brother said, "I have developed the ability to take a bone and put flesh on it." "Is that so?" the second brother said. "I have developed the ability to take a bone with flesh on it and put skin and fur on it as well." "And I," chimed in the third brother, "have developed the ability to take a bone with flesh and fur on it and create limbs." The fourth brother then jumped in and said, "I can take that limb with bone and skin and fur and give it life." And so the four brothers went into the jungle and found the bone of a lion. The first brother put flesh on the bone and the second brother grew a hide and hair on it and the third gave it matching legs and the fourth gave life to the lion. With a roar the lion shook his mane, ate the four brothers, and disappeared into the jungle.

In the Sermon on the Mount, Jesus tells us that we have the ability to create that which can devour us. If we're not careful—if our priorities are not straight, money and possessions can make us feel very wealthy for a moment and then leave us head over heels in debt. We can fool ourselves into thinking that we are successful and yet that success can be both temporary and destructive.

Significant losses

That is why Jesus says in Matthew 6:19, "Do not store up for yourselves treasures on earth, where moth and vermin destroy, and where thieves break in and steal" (NIV). Jesus tells us that earthly treasure is here today and gone tomorrow. For one thing—all earthly treasure will wear out and lose its value. That is a truth that Ross Perot, technology tycoon and one time U.S. presidential candidate, understands. He writes:

> Just remember, if you get real lucky, if you make a lot of money, if you go out and buy a lot of stuff—it's gonna break. You get your biggest, fanciest mansion in the world. It's got air conditioning. It's got a pool. Just think of all the pumps that are going to go out. Or go to a yacht basin any place in the world. Nobody is smiling, and I'll tell you why. Something broke that morning. The generator's out; the microwave oven doesn't work. . . . Things just don't mean happiness.[2]

There's something else here—in our terror-filled world our possessions can disappear in a heartbeat. In the wake of the September 11, 2001, tragedy, Martin Weber wrote these memorable words:

> So this is what it all comes down to . . . Ashes.
> Gigahertz computers and wireless uplinks,
> mahogany boardrooms and executive washrooms,
> leather portfolios and power lunch clubs . . .
> Everything amounts to ashes.
> Corporate strategies and market share,
> stock prices and interest rates,
> quarterly profits or losses . . .
> The bottom line is ashes.
> Office policies and politics,
> promotions and retirement plans,
> Brooks Brothers suits and the bodies inside . . .

All end up in ashes.
It's not the economy, after all. It's the ashes.
Save us, O God, from our ashes.[3]

But it's more than just possessions and wealth—there's the wear and tear on our souls—our spiritual lives. We work ourselves to death to get the "good life," and then we are too tired to enjoy it. We wheel and deal and climb the corporate or professional ladder on the backs of our colleagues and then wonder why it is so lonely at the top. We ride the stock market yo-yo up and down, up and down, and then wonder why we feel so strung out. We spend the whole day running a business and have no time or energy for the family. We trust our children to be raised by TV programs and the kids down the street. We give our ambitions everything we've got, and there's nothing left for God, church, mission, or spiritual life.

The Bible wants us to remember one more reality—in the end it's going to all burn up. On Judgment Day when every earthly thing is swept away, it's all going to burn up. And everything we thought was important won't be worth anything. That's why Jesus tells us in Matthew 6:20, 21, "Store up for yourselves treasures in heaven, where moths and vermin do not destroy, and where thieves do not break in and steal. For where your treasure is, there your heart will be also" (NIV).

Jesus is telling us to invest everything we have, all that we are, in the things that really matter.

Jesus wants us to put our time, money, and selves into the cause of Christ, because in the end that is the only thing that's going to matter. Let me suggest three very practical ways we can do that.

Invest in people

First of all, invest in people—especially hurting people. There are people all across town—or perhaps even neighbors—who have been laid low by the hard knocks of life. People who have never had a chance. People who have lost every-thing to a fire or have had their life savings swallowed up by a medical crisis. People who have been abandoned by the sole breadwinner in the family. People who have moved here from another country with big dreams and high hopes, but limited resources. And when we invest in hurting people, we invest in heaven. We become a tangible part of God's love working in their lives.

I heard about a woman in Denver known by many as the "Shoe Lady." One day in 1986, she was behind a shoe store where she found hundreds of new shoes in the dumpster. She piled the shoes into her car and took them to a homeless shelter. There she saw a pregnant woman walking through the shelter in her stocking feet. When she asked the person in charge why the woman wasn't wearing any shoes, he said, "Because we don't have any that fit her." After hearing that comment, the "Shoe Lady" developed a plan. She found out where all the shoe stores in town were located, every few days checked the dumpsters, took those shoes that were thrown out, and delivered them to shelters, churches, and other char-itable organizations. One day when she was at the shelter, her fifteen-year-old son saw a boy who needed something warm to wear. You can imagine the thrill that filled her heart when she saw her boy take off his own coat and give it to the boy shiv-ering in the cold. The lesson: this lady is not only investing in heaven by giving people shoes for the journey of life, she is helping the next generation capture the vision of serving Christ by serving others. How are we investing in people?

Invest in your church

Second, invest in your church. Now let's be very clear about something here—the church is more than bricks and pews, heat and lights, or the kitchen and paper towels. The church is people—people God has called to be His. And God calls us to invest in people who need our support in their spiritual journey. People who need friends to help them become fully devoted friends of Jesus Christ. Yes, it takes bricks, pews, tables, heat, lights, classrooms, materials, staffing, volunteers, and money to get the job done. When you give to the church budget, it is not only an act of worship; it is an important way of resourcing the ministries of our church. When we are not faithful stewards, the church cannot fulfill its mission. But when we are faithful stewards and share our resources, we can fulfill the mission God has given us. Faithful stewards invest in their churches.

Invest in the mission of the church

And that leads us to our third point—investing in heaven by investing in local evangelism and world mission. This is God's church, and we have a God-given assignment to accomplish the mission of the church. We are here to make disciples for Christ. Evangelism, bringing our families and friends to Jesus Christ, is central to the mission of the church. When we make friends with our neighbors and the people we meet at the health club and the folks we serve in the community, we build bridges to their hearts. We need the church to host events we can bring our friends to—concerts, socials, recovery groups, Bible study groups, health education seminars, and all the rest. It takes all of us working and giving together so that the church has resources to get the job done.

But the mission of the church is not just local—it's worldwide. The Seventh-day Adventist Church has spread throughout the world, because our system focuses on more than just the local congregation. We are privileged to support outreach throughout the world. Just think—the tithe and offerings we give in our local churches are shared worldwide. It's possible that before your congregation existed, offerings by church members from other congregations supported evangelism in your community. This system truly makes us a worldwide movement.

Conclusion

Years ago when we were a one-car family, I would get myself ready for church and some Sabbath mornings wait in the car. One of those mornings while I was waiting, a thought came to my mind: *We are a one-car family and the only way we are getting to church is if we go together.* And so if I wanted to speed up the process, I needed to help the rest of my family get ready to go. And then another thought came to my mind: *You might say that is the way it is in the church—the church is also a one-car family.* We need to go to heaven together—as a church family. And so we need to help each other get ready. We're all in this together. When we return tithes and give offerings—both local and abroad—we are investing in heaven. After all, that's where our hearts are—not here, but there.

David Livingstone, the well-known missionary, gave his life in mission service for Christ in Africa. When he died, his body was taken to England and buried in Westminster Abbey. But at the request of the people in Africa, his heart was buried in Africa. His heart is in the land where he was a missionary and with the people he loved so dearly.

I wonder, Where is your heart? I have to ask myself, Where is my heart? Where is our treasure? My prayer is that our life investment not be in stocks, real estate, or other places, but in the bank of heaven. Our investments in heaven will always be safe, and always yield a rich return. That's the assurance God gives us.

Endnotes

1. Bill Hybels, "Preaching for Total Commitment," *Leadership* (X:3), Summer 1989, 38.

2. Craig Brian Larson, *Illustrations for Preaching and Teaching* (Grand Rapids, Mich.: Baker Books, 1993), 151.

3. Martin Weber, "It's the Ashes," *Adventist Review,* January 3, 2002.

"X" Marks the Spot

Jeff Metherell

I remember, as a child, how thrilled I was when either a parent or teacher said, "Today, we are going to have a treasure hunt." A treasure hunt could end up being wonderfully rewarding or tantalizingly mysterious. In fact, if I ponder the notion of a treasure hunt, it quickly conjures up images from Robert Louis Stevenson's *Treasure Island*. I checked out this book from the library as a young boy and voraciously consumed it—images of loud-mouthed parrots and swashbuckling, bloodthirsty pirates intoxicated with dreams of buried treasure. So, today—please try to contain your excitement—we're going on a treasure hunt.

So, where is this treasure? Open your Bibles to Luke 12:34. Reading from the New King James Version, Jesus says, "Where your treasure is, there your heart will be also." Like any good treasure hunter, let's take a moment to analyze this clue. It sounds to me as if Jesus is saying, "If you want to find the treasure, first locate your heart, and that's where your treasure will be too." And, if you want to find where your heart is, look and see what it is that you really treasure in your life. It's like an equation, isn't it? Treasure equals heart; heart equals treasure.

"X" marks the spot where we'll find the treasure.

Perhaps this is why so many people have such a hard time surrendering their hearts to Jesus. They may want to, but it's hard to do. They say all the right words in their prayers; but, ultimately, they are frustrated and betrayed by the truth of this mathematical equation—heart equals treasure, and treasure equals heart. And "X" marks the spot. Turn to Matthew 19, and you'll read a story that most likely you have read before. But like a lot of biblical stories, there are truths below the surface—just like buried treasure—truths that all too often escape us. I am referring to the story of the rich young ruler. You remember the story—the young man asks Jesus what good thing he must do to get eternal life. Jesus tells him to obey the commandments, and the young man tells Jesus that he keeps the commandments. Finally, Jesus tells him to sell everything and give the proceeds to the poor. But as I study this story, I don't believe that Jesus was really asking the rich young ruler to surrender all of his worldly accumulations. He is asking for much more—Jesus is asking the young man to surrender his heart. Jesus knew that the man's heart was all wrapped up in his "stuff"—the things of this world. A Bible commentator states that the young man was "crestfallen," and walked away (Matthew 19:22, *The Message*). In other words, he was holding on tight to a lot of things—things, he couldn't let go of. We generally refer to this man as the rich young ruler, right? We might as well call him the foolish young ruler for the way he acted.

It's tempting to be critical of the rich young ruler. It's easy to call his decision foolish, but each of us needs to ask how we would have acted. Would we have walked away? What choice would we have made? We cannot detour around those questions.

Back to the treasure hunt

Let's go back to our treasure hunt. Usually, in the "treasure island" type of stories, there is one pirate who stands out as a diabolical character. He is the one who knows all about the treasure, where it is buried, and, of course, doesn't want anyone else to find it. This pirate comes across as murderous and sneaky, one who has no heart at all. In many ways, this character fits the description of Satan, doesn't he? This bad pirate does everything he can to keep would-be treasure hunters from even getting into the hunt. If this diabolical character can keep the other treasure hunters distracted, they pose little threat to ever finding the buried treasure. That's the way many hidden treasure stories are written. But, before you think it's just a story, this story may well describe how Satan acts. Satan doesn't really have to worry about us finding the treasure when we're distracted with our own selfish needs. We're not even in the hunt. We're neutralized. Sadly, we often have a very false perception of our own condition. "Why do I need to go and hunt for some buried treasure? Look at me. I've got it all!" Revelation 3:17 has a response to this self-absorbed spiritual arrogance, "You say, 'I am rich. I have everything I want. I don't need a thing!' And you don't realize that you are wretched and miserable and poor and blind and naked" (NLT).

But even if we are ready to hunt for that priceless treasure, we have another problem—we have the wrong treasure map. You and I may possess the enthusiasm and commitment, but we're looking in the wrong place. This is another common occurrence in "treasure island" type of stories. In these stories, the crafty and evil pirate gives the other pirates the wrong map—what a smart move. The duped buccaneers follow the instructions carefully, marking off the right number of paces from the coconut palm, digging in the right spot, only to uncover a treasure chest full of sand or the bones of other deceived treasure hunters.

Questions we must ask

What about us? Why do we let that crafty, evil pirate called Satan pawn off on us the wrong map? And how does he do that? For one thing, he distorts the truth about heaven. For most people, heaven has become more of a cartoon than a reality. Too many people think heaven is a place where people float on a cloud and strum a harp. What a warped concept of heaven. In Billy Joel's popular song from the 1970s, "Only the Good Die Young," you find these lyrics:

> They say there's a heaven for those who will wait.
> Some say it's better, but I say it ain't.
> I'd rather laugh with the sinners than cry with
>   the saints,
> the sinners are much more fun.
> You know that only the good die young.[1]

Add to this not-so-subtle message the scores of television programs and movies that trivialize heaven, and it's no wonder so many people today are deceived into believing that eternal life—as represented by heaven—isn't really much of a reward. Several years ago, a whimsical movie titled *Heaven Can Wait* told the far-fetched and theologically flawed story of a National Football League quarterback who, as a result of some bureaucratic error by his guardian angel, is whisked up to heaven following an accident. But, he doesn't *want* to be in heaven. So, for the remainder of the movie, he stubbornly negotiates with Mr. Jordan (God) to be allowed to return to earth—albeit in a different body since his was cremated before the mistake was discovered. All of this so he could play in the Super Bowl.

Now, I want you to contrast this sentiment—this value—with the words of Ellen White who, at the age of seventeen, was given her first vision that involved scenes of heaven. She writes,

> An angel bore me gently down to this dark world.
> Sometimes I think I can stay here no longer; all

things of earth look so dreary. I feel very lonely here, for I have seen a better land. Oh, that I had wings like a dove, then would I fly away and be at rest!

After I came out of vision, everything looked changed; a gloom was spread over all that I beheld. Oh, how dark this world looked to me. I wept when I found myself here, and felt homesick.[2]

That sounds like someone who has the right map. Her treasure wasn't the Super Bowl or anything on this earth. "X" marks the spot where both her treasure and her heart were.

Confusing us about heaven

I wish I could say that Satan is satisfied with making a parody of heaven. But he isn't. As usual, he goes for the knockout punch—he wants total victory. He not only puts down heaven, but he embellishes this earth and its attributes. This completely deceptive and utterly ruthless campaign has been going on for centuries. And the success of this strategy is clearly seen throughout history. For example, we see it as Lot's wife disobediently turned her head—her eyes magnetically drawn back to the sin-riddled city of Sodom, where her treasure and heart remained (Genesis 19). We see Satan's temporary victory in Nebuchadnezzar's boastful rant about the power and wealth of his kingdom before God's judgment eventually produces humility and new priorities (Daniel 4). We see it, of course, in the rich young ruler sadly walking away from Jesus, the "pearl of great price," who is standing in front of the young man, while blindly clutching to the possessions of a lost world. And we see it today in modern society's mad preoccupation with image, fashion, and status. The now familiar bumper sticker that reads "He who dies with the most toys wins," has truly become the credo of our age. Proverbs 15:16

counsels us, "Better is a little with the fear of the LORD than great treasure and turmoil with it" (NASB).

It is a testament to the matchless craft and guile of the enemy, that countless deceived people are, in essence, signing their names to the most lopsided contract imaginable. Throughout history, there have been some seriously senseless deals. Esau's bargain with his brother Jacob—a bowl of stew for his birthright blessing—clearly deserves a prominent place in the hall of fame (or hall of shame) for bad deals. On a much more trivial vein, in 1989 two football teams, the Dallas Cowboys and Minnesota Vikings, were involved in the largest player trade in the history of the National Football League. Herschel Walker, who was the centerpiece of this trade (often referred to as "the great train robbery"), was sent to the Vikings for a bounty of draft picks and players. This vastly lopsided trade is universally believed to have propelled the Cowboys into their dynasty years while the Vikings, by contrast, were mired, for the same number of years, in hopeless mediocrity. Friends, Satan is trying to get us to trade eternal life, basking in God's love and provision, without any trace of sickness, pain, or infirmity—for what? The deceiver is promising us the riches and pleasures of a dying world—currency that devalues; fast, beautiful cars that rust and fall into disrepair; fashionable and trendy clothing that fades and tears; pleasures that are fleeting at best and addictive and damaging at worst; cosmetic surgical enhancements performed on bodies soon to be returning to the dust from which they were created. The sad news is that many in this world are signing up for that trade. Read what the prophet Isaiah says: "Lift up your eyes to the heavens, look at the earth beneath; the heavens will vanish like smoke, the earth will wear out like a garment and its inhabitants die like flies. But my salvation will last forever, my righteousness will never fail" (Isaiah 51:6, NIV).

We need to be aware that the brainwashing is subtle and

cheap. It's like a harmful drink that we are asked to imbibe. It only appears delicious and quenching. It took the wisest man in the whole world a lifetime to discover that the gratification of this world, in spite of its initial lure, is ultimately meaningless. We should echo the prayer of the psalmist, who says,

> Turn my heart toward your statutes
> and not toward selfish gain (Psalm 119:36, NIV).

If you are wondering why this conference director of stewardship has been talking about treasure maps instead of appealing for sacrificial giving, here is the reason. God doesn't want your wallet. Just as with the rich young ruler, He wants your heart. He knows that "X" marks the spot. Where your treasure is, there will your heart be also. Our God can do anything, right? Almost, for He won't *make* anyone love Him. He won't *make* you give Him your heart. He could easily place a special "stewardship chip" in your brain so that every time an offering appeal was made, your hand just automatically reached for your purse or wallet. But He won't do that. He wants you to *give* Him your heart. And He knows that if you give Him your heart, you will be a good steward. Remember, heart equals treasure, treasure equals heart, and "X" marks the spot.

Jesus, when He was on this earth, was in many ways a revolutionary. He methodically attacked the deeply rooted religious misconceptions with the same passion that He lovingly healed the sick. Would you expect any different now? Doesn't it make sense that He would take aim at this current epidemic of materialism? Wouldn't He still be trying to teach and promote the heavenly value system as opposed to the counterfeit system of a dying world? The kingdom of heaven isn't built on the *gold* standard—it's built on the *love* standard.

I share with you a poem that I wrote a few years ago. It is called "Heaven's Gold."

Since time began, in human hearts
   Was born a frightful greed,
Which flourished and developed there
   'Til want determined need.

And wars were waged and blood was spilled
   And lives were bought and sold.
While people failed to realize
   That love is heaven's gold.

Image—now the holy grail,
   Is modern man's crusade.
We battle in Armani suits
   For things that rust and fade.

Still where we live and how we dress
   Is what we are we're told.
Our money's in the wrong account
   For love is heaven's gold.

And sadly, most are still consumed
   With legacies of wealth.
While sacrificing all that counts—
   Relationships and health.

Oft death has come with treasures clutched
   In hands now stiff and cold.
Just wasted life without the truth
   That love is heaven's gold.

The age-old quest continues yet
   While earthly riches pale.
And mortal efforts to succeed
   Are soon ordained to fail.

How blessed those few enlightened ones
  Who in their hearts now hold
That treasure without price or peer—
  For love is heaven's gold.

I admit that it's been kind of fun using a little creative license about treasure hunts with pirate imagery. But I hope you understand that the stark reality of this issue is not about a ride at an entertainment park. The stakes are high. We're talking about eternal life versus eternal nonexistence. Jesus tells us, "Do not store up for yourselves treasures on earth, where moth and rust destroy, and where thieves break in and steal. But store up for yourselves treasures in heaven, where neither moth nor rust destroys, and where thieves do not break in or steal; for where your treasure is, there your heart will be also" (Matthew 6:19–21, NASB).

Endnotes

1. http://www.sing365.com/music/lyric.nsf/Only-The-Good-Die-Young -lyrics-Billy-Joel/956D520953E906A248256870001B64DD (accessed February 11, 2013).

2. Ellen G. White, *Early Writings of Ellen G. White* (Washington, D.C.: Review and Herald®, 1945), 20.

Knowledge, Commitment, and Transformation—

the Making of a Faithful Steward

Domingo Paulino

As Christians, we have the opportunity to listen to sermons, read books such as the Bible, or attend seminars on topics like stewardship. Stewardship materials encourage us to put into practice the principles learned and invite us to make pledges to the Lord as faithful stewards. Many of us respond to these calls and see the blessings in our personal lives as well as in the life of our congregation. The tithe as well as the offerings begin to increase. The local and general needs of the church are met. The morale is high because the funds are flowing into the Lord's storehouse. Projects are started and completed; financial reports are encouraging. The future looks bright and promising. We are confident that as long as the people understand and practice what they are taught about the principles of stewardship, everything will be all right.

However, as time goes by, we often notice that we go back to our previous predicament. Pledges are broken, tithe and offerings are down, and morale is low. The situation is worse because a new element has been added—guilt. People feel that they have not been faithful to their vows to the Lord and many feel terrible about it. As leaders, we try to alleviate the situation by making appeals, giving more information, holding business meetings to report on the crisis. However, the situation does not seem to change or improve. We start asking ourselves what went wrong. We begin looking for scapegoats and question the leaders or the people's faithfulness. The outcome can be total disillusionment, and the survival mode takes control again.

As a pastor, I have witnessed this situation a number of times. After much prayer and analysis of this issue, I have come to the conclusion that the cause for this problem does not lie in the lack of communication or information about stewardship. Neither is it due to a lack of enthusiasm of our church members to be better stewards. Nor is the problem an absence of sincerity and honesty on the part of those who made a commitment and vow to the Lord. I believe that there are two reasons for this difficulty.

One reason is the belief that the presentation of information, manifestation of enthusiasm, and presence of sincerity are sufficient to produce and secure an enduring and unchangeable commitment to stewardship.

The other reason is the idea that an event such as a sermon, seminar, or a weeklong treatment of the stewardship subject is enough to transform a person into a solid steward.

These are good and necessary approaches to good stewardship, but there is still a missing element—discipline. We don't learn discipline overnight by attending a seminar or listening to a sermon. We don't create discipline on the spot by making a commitment or taking a vow. Discipline takes time—it is a learning process.

To help us understand and develop discipline, I propose that we learn from those who took the Nazirite vow as presented in Numbers 6. We do not often hear about the Nazirite vow, but we can learn from it. We can learn lessons about stewardship that will enable us to have a positive view of God's creation, its resources, and how to manage them according to God's plans. There are three aspects of stewardship that were part of the Nazirite vow— knowledge, commitment, and transformation.

Knowledge

A person did not take the Nazirite vow lightly. Specific external and internal conditions influenced their decision. The knowledge of God's purpose for the people of Israel was central. The story of Abraham and his descendants, the captivity and liberation from Egypt, the miracles in the desert, the law, and the sanctuary identified God's relationship with His people. God called them to be His. On the other hand, they were aware of the nation's failures in fulfilling God's purposes and the corruption in the priesthood. Most Israelites knew God's expectation and, at the same time, the people's shortcomings. In spite of that, God reminded the Israelites of the special relationship between Him and His people.

> Ye have seen what I did unto the Egyptians,
> and how I bare you on eagles' wings, and brought
> you unto myself. Now therefore, if ye will obey
> my voice indeed, and keep my covenant, then
> ye shall be a peculiar treasure unto me above all
> people: for all the earth is mine: And ye shall be
> unto me a kingdom of priests, and an holy nation
> (Exodus 19:4–6, KJV).

God called His people to holiness, both the nation and the individuals. Even if the majority in the nation turned their backs on God, it was still the responsibility of each individual to be faithful to God. When the majority of the people of Israel rebelled at Mount Sinai, God still called the Levites to be His servants. God chose them to serve, even when they became corrupted, God still chose individuals like Samuel to be His servants. Each individual was accountable to God, and that was a key factor in the decision to become a Nazirite.

The principle of personal accountability still applies today—we are called to be holy. Peter says, "You are a chosen people, a royal priesthood, a holy nation, a people to be his very own and to proclaim the wonderful deeds of the one who called you out of darkness into his marvelous light" (1 Peter 2:9, ISV).

God has chosen and blessed His church in order to make her a light. We are called to be stewards of God's richness in this world, but everyone does not respond. We participate in stewardship seminars and listen to stewardship sermons in order to learn how to be faithful stewards. While many in this world are choosing not to be faithful stewards, God's people respond joyfully. They see themselves as stewards of God's resources.

While knowledge was important to those taking the Nazirite vow, it does not stop with knowledge. Commitment was also needed.

Commitment

When my wife and I were buying a home, the attorney handling the paperwork explained to us why we had to sign so many documents. He told us that his first closing was more than forty years ago, and at that closing only one document had to be signed—the loan document. Over the years, he told us, more and more people defaulted on their loans and the banks required the signing of more documents. It seemed to him that people's commitments to pay the loan decreased over the years. The challenge is not that people don't know what they need to do—commitment calls for sacrifice and that's why some people find it difficult to fulfill their commitments.

The person who took the Nazirite vow not only had knowledge, but also the willingness to sacrifice. For example, the individual was separated from daily activities in order to deepen their relationship with God. All other activities were secondary—God was the priority. Each person made a personal commitment.

The Israelites, while traveling to the Promised Land, all too often looked back fondly to Egypt, as if life had been good there. At the same time, they were in danger of falling to the idolatrous practices of the Canaanites. Today, we are surrounded by a materialistic society dominated by consumerism. We are constantly bombarded with media messages that put everything and everyone ahead of God. As with the Israelites, we are at risk of losing God's vision for our lives. It is a danger as old as the entrance of sin into this world. The difference is that today things are magnified and widely spread by mass media. Jesus' words are as true today as they were when He first pronounced them: "No man can serve two masters: for either he will hate the one, and love the other; or else he will hold to the one, and despise the other. Ye cannot serve God and mammon" (Matthew 6:24, KJV).

Later in the same discourse, this appeal was made: "Seek ye first the kingdom of God, and his righteousness; and all these things shall be added unto you" (verse 33, KJV).

This was exactly what the person who took the Nazirite vow did—he made a commitment to put God first and above everything and everyone. How do you exercise that kind of commitment? There are at least three ways:

First, set aside specific time for the purpose of consecrating totally and exclusively to God. The amount of time may not be the same, but each of us needs to set aside this special time.

Second, adopt a lifestyle characterized by total abstinence of bad things, things that are harmful to our spiritual
development.

And finally, remember specific events in our spiritual journey that help us renew our commitment to God.

Transformation

We have focused on the importance of knowledge and commitment, and now we focus on the outcome—transformation.
Transformation occurs because of the knowledge we obtain
and the commitment we make. Transformation is part of our
sanctification process, and this transformation has a lot to do
with our stewardship.

Those who took the Nazirite vows help us see what it
means to experience transformation. The behavior of those
who took the vow changed dramatically. For example, their
behavior after the death of a loved one was governed. The Bible states, "He shall not make himself unclean for his father,
or for his mother, for his brother, or for his sister, when they
die: because the consecration of his God is upon his head"
(Numbers 6:7, KJV). This was emotionally difficult to fulfill
but the individuals who took the vow did it. What was the
basis for this behavior? Even though they experienced pain
when a loved one died, it was a practical fulfillment of Deuteronomy 6:5: "And thou shalt love the LORD thy God with
all thine heart, and with all thy soul, and with all thy might"
(KJV). Their comfort came from God and not from partici-
pating in the funeral of a loved one.

Another example of how their lives were changed has to
do with what they drank. The consumption of wine or any
product of the vine was, and still is, associated with banquets,
parties, and social gatherings. Wine is a social drink. What's
wrong with a banquet or party? Nothing intrinsically, however, for a Nazirite it was a potentially dangerous place or environment. Job offered sacrifices for his sons and daughters

after they had their banquets just in case they had offended God (Job 1:5). We know that Samson violated his vows when he touched the dead body of a lion. We don't know if he drank wine or any product of the vine, but he participated in banquets and social activities with the Philistines. The Nazirite was not asked to practice moderation, but rather abstinence. The mind of the individual was the first target of the devil. The body was still craving for those things that the vow excluded; however, the mind was in control. The goal was that, at the end of the process of change, the physical and emotional aspects of the individual were aligned and functioning harmoniously with reason. There was no place for indulgence. Only after the Nazirites fulfilled certain conditions were they allowed to practice moderation again (Numbers 6:19, 20).

And finally, even the outward appearance of those who took the vow was transformed. The Bible states, "After [the Nazirite] has shaved his dedicated hair . . . " (verse 19, NASB), the priest was to continue with the offering of the sacrifice. Even though the Bible does not mention what the social norm for the length of the hair in a man or woman was at that time, the vow of the Nazirite to God overruled any social requirement or norm in this regard.

These three examples show the radical transformation that took place in the lives of those who took the Nazirite vows. As radical as they are, these examples teach us valuable lessons and principles about our duties as stewards of God's resources. Those who took the vows experienced a radical change in their lives. But such radical changes occur even outside religious lives. Think of the Olympic athletes. They often abstain from many things—even legitimate things. They do whatever it takes to be winners. If athletes make such deep commitments to their sport, what should we as followers of Jesus Christ do?

The best example

Transformation requires commitment, and those who took the Nazirite vows or the athletes are good examples of commitment. But there is another example that will help us make that commitment in our lives. That is the example of Jesus Christ and how He was victorious over the temptations He experienced.

When the devil tempted Jesus to turn stones into bread, Jesus replied, "The Scriptures say: 'No one can live only on food. People need every word that God has spoken' " (Matthew 4:4, CEV).

When the devil challenged Jesus to throw Himself from the temple, Jesus responded with, "The Scriptures also say, 'Don't try to test the Lord your God!' " (verse 7, CEV).

And finally, when the devil tempted Jesus with the kingdoms of this world, Jesus told the devil, "Go away Satan! The Scriptures say: 'Worship the Lord your God and serve only him' " (verse 10, CEV).

Conclusion

What can we learn from those who took the Nazirite vows? What can we learn from Jesus' victory of temptations?

We learn that knowledge is important. That knowledge comes from God's Word, our prayer life, and the leading of the Holy Spirit. Jesus responded to the devil's temptations with words from the Bible. If you and I know the Word of God, we can be spiritually strong.

We learn that commitment follows knowledge. The Nazirites made a commitment to put God first in their lives. Jesus did not allow the things of this world to be first in His life—He committed His life to fulfilling His mission.

Finally, we learn that transformation comes because Jesus Christ changes our lives. Without Jesus Christ, knowledge has no value. Without Jesus Christ, commitment is not possible. But, with Jesus Christ, we are transformed.

A transformed person is a faithful steward. Faithful stewards are not individuals who try harder—faithful stewards are individuals whose lives have been transformed. Once our lives are transformed, we are faithful with our time, talents, and possessions. We are not faithful stewards because of fear, but because transformation enables us to practice radical stewardship in our lives. We become God's disciplined stewards on this earth.

Trusting God

Orlando Rosales

Without any fanfare, the prophet Elijah is introduced in 1 Kings 17:1–16. The Bible only tells us that he was from Tishbe, a town in Gilead. Elijah was delivering a message to King Ahab. Ahab's queen was the infamous Jezebel, and we are told that Ahab did evil in the sight of the Lord (1 Kings 16:30). It was to this king that Elijah announced there would be neither rain nor dew—a negative message to a king who did not worship God.

How was Elijah able to deliver such a message to a king who did not worship the God of heaven? It's because he was doing God's mission. Whenever we do God's mission, He gives us power to fulfill it. It is not a power we possess; rather, God enables us to do it. We obtain that power by developing a personal relationship with God. Because of that relationship, we obey God with confidence, without reservations, and without fear.

Elijah's messages must have stunned the king and, no doubt, angered him. It's not what the king wanted to hear. Even though Ba'al, one of Ahab's gods, was considered to be the god of rain and fruitfulness, Ahab did not want to hear the news from Elijah. The king was facing a test: Who was the true God? Was it the God of Israel, or Ba'al? Even though Ahab worshiped Ba'al, he may have known about the true God and realized that Ba'al was not able to help.

Elijah in Kerith

After Elijah delivered the devastating message to Ahab, God sent Elijah on another mission. God tells Elijah, "Leave here, turn eastward and hide in the Kerith Ravine, east of the Jordan. You will drink from the brook, and I have directed the ravens to supply you with food there" (1 Kings 17:3, 4, NIV). God gives Elijah specific instructions and even tells the prophet how he will survive there. Elijah probably knew brook Kerith well and, as a child, may have played near the brook, located near the River Jordan. Though the brook was known, the journey there was strenuous, but once he was there, he was removed from angry king Ahab. Ahab was not there, but God was, providing, through the ravens, food in the morning and in the evening. Elijah's drinking water came from the seasonal brook that carried its water to the River Jordan.

During the time Elijah lived by the brook, he entered into a trusting relationship with God. He may not have fully understood God's plan, but he trusted God with his life. That's the way God wants us to live. Jesus invites us to have a relationship of trust with God. He tells us, "Seek first his kingdom and his righteousness, and these things will be given to you as well" (Matthew 6:33, NIV). Jesus is an example of trusting God.

Elijah's food was supplied until a crisis came—the brook dried up because there was no rain. The very thing Elijah told Ahab—that there would be no rain or dew—was fulfilled. What was he to do? Where would he go? Would God supply his needs, or would Ahab find him and punish him? These are the questions that came to his mind as he looked into a bleak future.

Elijah in Zarephath

God had another plan for Elijah—an unexpected plan. He tells Elijah, "Go at once to Zarephath in the region of Sidon and stay there. I have directed a widow there to supply you with food" (1 Kings 17:9, NIV). God's command was unexpected, and it did not seem very promising—his food was to come from a widow. First, Elijah is told to go to Zarephath in the Sidon region. He had to travel more than fifty miles and, in his day, that was a long and hard journey. Zarephath, a coastal town on the Mediterranean Sea, was also in the center of Ba'al worship. It was not too long before that Elijah confronted King Ahab, a worshiper of Ba'al, and now God tells Elijah to go to a town in the center of Ba'al worship. Elijah's journey did not sound like a promising journey for a prophet in need of food.

As if the destination was not strange, God tells Elijah to get his food from a person who probably did not have much food. He says to Elijah, "I have directed a widow there to supply you with food" (verse 9, NIV). God does not choose a rich owner of land or flocks of sheep to feed Elijah—instead He tells Elijah that a widow will provide his food. In those days, probably more so than in today's culture, widows had great difficulty surviving. They depended on handouts from family and friends. Getting enough food was always a problem, and yet God tells Elijah that his food would come from a widow. I wonder what thoughts went through Elijah's mind as he traveled westward to his new destination.

Elijah obeyed God, not because he understood but because God had spoken. Up to that point, God had provided food through the ravens. That was not a promising plan either, but it was what God had chosen to do. Surely, Elijah must have thought, *If God is asking me to go to a widow, God will provide.* Every step Elijah took was a step of faith.

Almost matter-of-factly, the Bible tells us, "So he went to Zarephath" (verse 10, NIV). When he came to the town, village elders or other important citizens did not greet him. Rather, the first person he saw was a widow gathering sticks. Obviously, she was not a rich person—a rich person would not be gathering sticks. But God gave Elijah a specific command— he was told to go to this town and ask a widow for food.

The Bible tells us that when he met the widow, he did not ask for food. Rather, he said to her, "Would you bring me a little water in a jar so I may have a drink?" (verse 10, NIV). Was it a lack of faith that prevented him from asking for the food? Was it a desire not to burden a poor woman with a request for food? Or was it because he was thirsty from his long journey? We don't know, but what we do know is that as she was walking to get the water, Elijah finally spoke his bold request: "And bring me, please, a piece of bread" (verse 11, NIV).

I imagine Elijah was surprised to hear the request for bread leave his lips. The woman, though, must have been shocked, because she knew her situation better than Elijah. Her response tells us something of her desperate condition: "I don't have any bread—only a handful of flour in a jar and a little oil in a jug. I am gathering a few sticks to take home and make a meal for myself and my son, that we may eat it—and die" (verse 12, NIV).

This is a picture of hopelessness. A desperate prophet traveled many miles and asked a widow to give him water and bread. A hopeless widow who did not have enough food for her son and herself is asked to give bread to the prophet. The situation could not be worse. Yet the story unfolds unexpectedly. Elijah, we would expect, would apologize and tell the widow he was sorry for even asking. Perhaps in his mind he is thinking that he must be asking the wrong widow. Surely God did not send him on an arduous journey to ask for food from a widow who had enough oil and flour for only one meal.

Instead of apologizing for his request, Elijah is bold. He

asks the widow to go and make the bread, but *first* for Elijah and *only then* for her son and herself. Yet, this unusual request is preceded by a promise. Elijah tells the widow, "Don't be afraid" (verse 13, NIV). And why not be afraid? Is it that Elijah possessed some personal power? Not at all—it's because it's a promise from "the God of Israel" (verse 14, NIV). Elijah tells the widow that the oil will not run dry nor will the flour be used up until the Lord gives rain. Elijah, the widow, and her son would survive because God will provide.

This is a story of faith—a test of faith. Elijah's faith was tested. He went on a journey trusting God—he asked the widow for food. And now the widow's faith was tested. What would she do? What would you and I have done? We *read* the story, but the woman was not reading the story—she was *experiencing* the events.

I remember reading this story in the well-known Bible storybook written by Arthur S. Maxwell.[1] The writer portrays this story in a very dramatic way. As I recall, he wrote that the widow was kneading the bread, and her child was next to her, hurrying her because he was hungry. While the bread is baking, her impatient son asks, "How much longer?" Meanwhile, Elijah's words "give me first" echo in the mother's head. What does she tell the boy? What is the woman thinking?

The widow was facing a dilemma that many of us face. We often have to make decisions that are difficult to make. On one hand, we have needs, and yet we are told that our needs do not come first. The widow, we are told, "did as Elijah had told her" (verse 15, NIV). But it was not just because the prophet asked her; rather, it was because she was convinced that God had "spoken by Elijah" (verse 16, NIV). God's requests are sometimes hard to understand, but when God asks us to do something, it is always safe to follow His requests.

The widow did not know the outcome of her act of faith. The Lord not only provided bread for the prophet, but He also provided bread for the widow and her son. And the bread God provided for the widow and her son was not the last meal; rather, it was the beginning of ongoing blessings. Instead of finding enough flour and oil for the last meal, the Bible tells us, " 'The jar of flour will not be used up and the jug of oil will not run dry until the day the LORD sends rain on the land' " (verse 14, NIV). The Lord blessed the widow beyond her expectations.

We may not be asked to share our last bread with someone, but we are tested just as that widow was. How often have you heard these words? " 'Bring the whole tithe into the storehouse, that there may be food in my house. Test me in this,' says the LORD Almighty, 'and see if I will not throw open the floodgates of heaven and pour out so much blessing that there will not be room enough to store it' " (Malachi 3:10, NIV).

When you hear these words, what is your reaction? Some may say that it is just not possible to fulfill God's call for tithe. Some of us think that one day in the future we will be faithful and return the Lord's tithe, but right now we just can't do it. The reality is that tithing is a challenge unless we have a trusting relationship with God. God asks us to be faithful, and at the same time God also promises to bless us. The next time you hear the passage from Malachi read, ask God to help you believe that He will be faithful and fulfill His promise to bless you.

Conclusion

What do we learn from this message? Elijah's experience helps us to understand what it means to trust God. God asked Elijah to deliver a message to King Ahab even though the king would be angry at the message. Elijah did what God asked him to do. God then told Elijah to travel to a brook near the River Jordan and wait there for his food. Ravens would bring the food God promised. Elijah lived from the food brought by the ravens and from drinking water from the brook. But then the brook dried up, and Elijah faced a crisis. God, almost matter-of-factly, told Elijah to travel west—all the way to the Mediterranean Sea—and there he would receive food. And who would provide the food? A widow. He obeyed God, and God fulfilled the promise He made.

And what about the widow? She was desperate because she had enough for just one meager meal—the last meal she and her son would ever eat. It was one thing for Elijah to ask for a drink of water, but what was she to do when the prophet asked for bread? What bread? The last bread that she would make for her son and herself? That's exactly what the prophet requested. Once the widow recognized God's hand in Elijah's request, she gave him the bread, and she and her son continued living because God provided.

Elijah and the widow experienced the blessing promised by the psalmist:

> I was young and now I am old,
>> yet I have never seen the righteous forsaken
>> or their children begging bread (Psalm 37:25, NIV).

What about us—can we experience the same blessings? Just as God asked Elijah and the widow to make Him first, He asks us to do the same. But to put God first means that we have to have faith, and that is not always easy. Often our faith is overtaken by fear. But if we allow fear to control us, we will not be faithful stewards. So, what do we do? Through study of the Word and prayer, we need to develop a relationship of trust with God. Once we have such a relationship with God, we will have faith. Once we have faith, we will put God first, and God will care for us.

He fulfilled His promise to Elijah. He fulfilled His promise to the widow, and He will fulfill His promise to each of us.

God never fails us.

Endnote

1. Arthur S. Maxwell, *The Bible Story* (Hagerstown, Md.: Review and Herald®), 5:22, 23.

Does God Need My Money?

Robin Song

I invite you to listen to the reading from God's Word.

> "Bring the whole tithe into the storehouse, so that there may be food in My house, and test Me now in this," says the LORD of hosts, "if I will not open for you the windows of heaven and pour out for you a blessing until it overflows" (Malachi 3:10, NASB).

The late pastor W. A. Criswell shares a story of a young man who told his pastor that he would promise God a tithe of his income. The pastor and the young man prayed for God to bless his career. At that time the man was making $40.00 a week, and so he tithed $4.00. In a few years, his income increased dramatically, and he was *tithing* $500.00 per week. The day came when the man asked the pastor to see if he could be *released* from his tithing promise, because it was too much money now. The pastor replied, "I don't see how you can be *released* from your promise, but we can ask God to reduce your income to $40.00 a week; then you'd have no problem tithing $4.00."[1]

The well-known billionaire, J. D. Rockefeller, one of the richest men in history, helps us understand what happened with the young man who wanted to be released from his tithing commitment. Rockefeller said, "I never would have been able to tithe the first million dollars I ever made, if I had not tithed my first salary that was $1.50 per week."[2]

The question for you and me is this: What is it about tithing that's so difficult? Why is it that giving 10 percent of a small amount is much easier to give than 10 percent of a large amount? Is it really easier to return tithe on a small amount, or is it that the individual never understood God's tithing plan to begin with?

Tithe

Our tithe is what we are asked to return to God—it's one-tenth of the amount God has blessed us with. In our culture and economic system, that usually means returning one-tenth of our income. In Bible times, tithing was often done differently. Then, as now, tithe was used for those who served God's people, but the people did not have a monetary system similar to ours.[3] God's people returned tithe in various ways. They returned fruit, grain, oil, and wine. People tithed all their produce and goods—it was to be a literal storehouse full of food for the priests to eat.

Today, in the Seventh-day Adventist Church, tithe is used similarly as in the Old Testament. The tithe is sent to the local conference and redistributed to finance all the pastors, evangelists, conference workers, Christian educators, and others in ministry work. It's a system that has been used by the Seventh-day Adventist Church from its early days and has worked well. One reason that our church has become a worldwide church is because of the tithing system.

Who's returning the tithe?

The problem, however, isn't really a matter of where the

tithe is going, but from where the tithe is coming. Studies by the Barna Group, a research group tracking spiritual development and trends in churches, have shown the percentage of born-again Christians who actually tithe is 9 percent.[4] That means 91 percent of born-again Christians do not tithe. Imagine: 91 percent are nontithers! This is a really big problem in the church. On top of that—it's the middle class—those making between $40,000 and $100,000 per year—that consistently return the least amount to God.[5] The poor—those making less than $20,000 per year—consistently give a much higher percentage of their income than people that make triple and even quadruple of what they make.[6] Like our illustration earlier—tithing is far more likely to happen when we're making $100 a week, as opposed to when we're making $1,000 a week. Studies also show that it's those of us over the age of forty-five who are 80 percent more likely to tithe than those under forty-five.[7] The younger you are, studies show, the less likely you are to tithe, especially if you're under twenty-five, or if you're a single young adult who's never been married. Researchers calculate 1 percent or less of that group returns tithe.[8]

Robbing God

These are sobering findings. It's obvious that a significant number of Christians do not return tithe. But what does it mean to not return tithe? Unfaithfulness in tithing is not only a problem in our age. It was a big problem in Bible times also. In Malachi 3:8, God asks, " 'Will a man rob God? Yet you are robbing Me!' " (NASB). Rob God? What are you talking about? I don't steal from God! That's the exact expression that God is expecting you to say, because the very next words we read in the Bible are, " 'But you say, "How have we robbed You?" In tithes and offerings.' " Now, you and I are immediately inclined to say, "Wait, what? How does that make sense? The money I make belongs to me, doesn't it? Everything I earn is rightfully mine, isn't it?" Yet what does Psalm 24:1 say? "The earth is the LORD's, and all its fullness, the world and those who dwell therein" (NJKV). In Haggai 2:8, God says, " 'The silver is Mine, and the gold is Mine,' says the LORD of hosts" (NKJV). Thus, everything we earn and we say belongs to us, God says, "Think again!" When we don't return our tithe to God, He says that we are breaking the eighth commandment by stealing from Him. Everything already belongs to God. He's only asking for a portion of what already belongs to Him. These are strong words, but we need to listen to them because they are from the Word of God.

Does God need my money?

So it seems it's a two-way street. We need God's blessings, but God needs our faithfulness too. After all, without the money that is returned to the church, we wouldn't have a church, would we? And it especially seems that way if you've ever heard the treasurer's report, or served as a member on church committees. We are told that God needs our money—or does He? Listen to Psalm 50:12: "If I were hungry I would not tell you, for the world is Mine, and all it contains" (NASB). Bear in mind—God is talking to His people in the Old Testament who regularly brought food, produce, and crops to Him. He's saying, "What do you think all this food that you're bringing into God's storehouse is for anyway? You think you're feeding God? You think I need your food to satisfy My hunger?" God says, "Even if I were hungry, I don't need you to feed Me—I'll feed Myself!"

That really throws us for a loop. You mean God doesn't need our money? Why am I giving my tithe if God doesn't need it?

A New Testament passage helps us understand what God is saying. Let us look at 2 Corinthians 9:7. Paul writes, "Each of you should give what you have decided in your heart to give" (NIV). But notice that we should give as our heart has decided—whether it's 2 percent, 10 percent, 50 percent, or even 0 percent. One more thing should characterize our giving—it should not be "reluctantly or under compulsion, for God loves a cheerful giver." If we give out of guilt or if we are reluctant, God says, Don't give!

Clearing up the confusion

Sounds somewhat confusing, doesn't it? On one hand, God wants the tithe—we can even say demands it. He says we're robbing Him if we don't return the tithe. On the other hand, God says He doesn't need anything from us. God is telling us that He loves the sincerity and generosity more than the actual amount. We will give sincerely and generously if we have a personal relationship with God—if we trust God. Our giving will be sincere and generous if we trust that God will care for us—that He will bless us. It has to be a relationship of trust. When we have a trusting relationship, we do not give because we have to, but because we are in partnership with God.

It's different with many other financial issues in our lives. For example, if we don't pay our electric, gas, or water bills, those needed services will most likely be cut off. If we don't pay our taxes, the government will take action to collect the taxes, and we may even have major legal issues. We know the consequences of not fulfilling our financial obligations, but God does not work the same way. God wants us to be willing givers. Returning tithe is a spiritual experience—an experience of joy.

My children

Whenever my two children hear that I am going somewhere by car, they volunteer to come with me. They're always eager to get out of the house, jump in the car, and go wherever Daddy is going. Every now and then they get hungry, and we'll stop by a fast-food restaurant or drive-thru for food. Usually we get sandwiches, a drink, and one order of French fries. Often I continue driving while we eat our food. I always divide the French fries between the two children. After we are on the road again, I ask my six-year-old son for a few French fries. He takes a few and passes them from the backseat to me. Then I'll ask my three-year-old daughter for a few French fries from her plate. She hands me a few French fries. A few minutes later, I repeat my requests—first to my son and then to my daughter. This goes on until the French fries are gone.

But that's not the way it was the first time I asked them for French fries. When I first asked my son, he gave me *one* French fry from his plate—that's it, one French fry. And my daughter—she did the same—one French fry. When I received one French fry, I would teasingly ask them why they gave me only one French fry. I told them I needed more than one. They laughed and gave me another fry.

That's the way our informal system worked until one day something different happened. Even before I asked for a French fry, one of the children said, "Here, Daddy—you want some French fries?" I did not have to ask. My child asked *me* if I wanted French fries—it was more than one.

The French fries my children *volunteered* to give me were the best ones I have ever eaten. My children chose to give me even before I asked.

I started thinking about "What if?" What if my kids had a different attitude toward the whole situation? What if they started whining uncontrollably when I asked them for French fries? What if my kids said, "Daddy, take your French fries as soon as we buy them in the restaurant so we know what's ours and what's yours"?

What if they said, "Don't give us all of the French fries and then ask us to give you some back. Why don't you just give us what is ours and you keep what is yours?"

Of course, if we did it that way, neither my children nor I would experience the joy of sharing.

The sharing God

Let's go back to Malachi 3:10 and read it again. God says, " 'Bring the whole tithe into the storehouse, that there may be food in my house. Test me in this,' says the LORD Almighty, 'and see if I will not throw open the floodgates of heaven and pour out so much blessing that there will not be room enough to store it' " (NIV). God invites us to test Him. God, our Creator and Redeemer, invites us to test Him. That's quite an invitation. And what is the outcome of that test? God says that He will bless us, and we never have to worry about money. That's God's promise to us. This experience is so enjoyable for God that He can't wait to bless us—even more than we imagined.

After my children volunteered to share their food with me, I looked forward with anticipation to the next time we shared our food. That's the way God is. He wants to share with us. He looks forward to another joyful experience, and you and I are blessed by Him.

Appeal

Look at what you have in your hands. It doesn't have to just be your paycheck. Whether it's your paycheck, your birthday gift, or your lunch money that your mom gave you. There is Someone in the front seat at the steering wheel of your life who gave that to you, isn't there? Will you take a piece of that blessing and give it to the One at the steering wheel, and say, "Here, Daddy. Would You like some? This is for You." I know you're struggling. I know it can be really hard. But God says, "Test Me on this!" If I saw my son or daughter starving and they still willingly volunteered to give me their last French fry, I'd drive to a restaurant and get more fries. In fact, I would not get one order—I'd get a huge bucket of fries.

Wouldn't you do the same?

Wouldn't God do the same? That's exactly what God does for each of us.

Endnotes

1. W. A. Criswell, *Criswell's Guidebook for Pastors* (Nashville, Tenn.: B & H Publishing Group, 2000), 156.

2. Ibid., 154.

3. See Leviticus 27:30–32 and Numbers 18:20–32.

4. The Barna Group, "New Study Shows Trends in Tithing and Donating," http://www.barna.org/congregations-articles/41-new-study-shows -trends-in-tithing-and-donating (accessed April 2, 2013).

5. Tim Stafford, "The Anatomy of a Giver: American Christians Are the Nation's Most Generous Givers, but We Aren't Exactly Sacrificing," *Christianity Today,* May 19, 1997, via Web site: http://library.generousgiving .org/page.asp?sec=4&page=161 (accessed April 2, 2013).

6. George Barna, "Evangelicals Are the Most Generous Givers, but Fewer Than 10 Percent of Born Again Christians Give 10 Percent to Their Church," news release by Barna Research Group, April 5, 2000, via Web site: http://library.generousgiving.org/page.asp?sec=4&page=161 (accessed April 2, 2013).

7. The Barna Group, "The Economy's Impact (Part 3 of 3): Donors Reduce Giving, Brace for the Long Haul," http://www.barna.org/barna-update /article/18-congregations/341-the-economys-impact-part-3-of-3-donors -reduce-giving-brace-for-the-long-haul.

8. The Barna Group, "New Study Shows Trends in Tithing and Donating," http://www.barna.org/congregations-articles/41-new-study-shows -trends-in-tithing-and-donating (accessed April 2, 2013).

Why We Bring the Tithe

Patrick Vincent

I invite you to hear God's words from Malachi 3:10:[1]

> Bring ye all the tithes into the storehouse, that
> there may be meat in mine house, and prove me now
> herewith, saith the LORD of hosts, if I will not open
> you the windows of heaven, and pour you out a bless-
> ing, that there shall not be room enough to receive it.

Our spotlight is on the first two words of this passage—"Bring ye." My sermon is about stewardship and is designed to clarify our understanding of why we do *what* we do. Why do we bring the tithe? What is the motivation? Why is it that many of you Sabbath after Sabbath faithfully bring tithe to the Lord's house?

About 45 percent of our members are regular tithers. Why do these individuals bring the tithe to the Lord? What is it that they know and experience that nontithers do not? Why do non-tithers not bring their tithe? What is it that they do not know and experience? What can we say about tithing so that all are impelled, propelled, and compelled to be tithers?

Why tithe?

Why do we bring the tithe? There are several biblical reasons why every blood-bought, born-again believer who has been blended into the body of Christ should bring the tithe.

The *first* reason is that we understand the command. Look again at Malachi 3:10. It says, "Bring ye." You will notice that this is not an option or suggestion. He did not say, "I suggest that you bring the tithe." He says, "Bring ye." That is a command. It is a command from God telling us how God wants us to support His work. Tithing is not a conference plan, local church plan, or the Christian's plan. It is God's plan.

Tithing is a very *sacred plan.* Anything that God gives us is sacred because it is of divine origin and comes directly from God. It is also a very *simple plan.* The word *tithe* means "tenth." Tithing is not as complicated as figuring out your income taxes. God says, divide your income into ten parts and bring one-tenth of your income for the Lord to support His work. God leaves it up to us what to do with the remaining nine-tenths.

Tithing is also a very *satisfying plan.* God says, when you do it, "I will open the windows of heaven and pour you out a blessing." Why does He say the windows and not the doors of heaven? I believe it's because heaven is pictured as God's house and a house always has more windows than it has doors. Usually, your house has a front door and back door, but there are windows in every room. God says, I am poised and waiting to open every window in heaven and pour you out a blessing so that you will not have enough room for it. When you do not have room enough to receive something, that means there will be an overflow to bless those in your concentric circle of contacts. So it is a simple, sacred, and satisfying plan.

Why follow God's plan?

There are three reasons why following God's plan is the best idea.

First, God *expects it*. He says, "Bring ye." He just says it and the implication is that He expects us to do it. Why would He command it if He did not expect us to do it? God expects it.

And then, God *explains it*. He tells us why He wants us to do it. He says, "that there may be meat in mine house." When God's people obey His command, there will be more than enough resources in God's house to do what He wants done. God expects it. God explains it.

And finally, God *encourages it*. He says, "prove me now herewith." That is a challenge from God to you. He says, Prove Me. He did not say to prove yourselves, rather prove God. That is where a lot of saints become disillusioned—they try to prove themselves. They sit down with a pencil and a piece of paper and they figure up their income and their out-go only to discover that there is too much month at the end of their money; and they say, "I don't think I am able to tithe." That is because those individuals have misread the command.

God did not say put yourself to the test. He said, Put Me to the test and see how much better off you will be with nine-tenths, plus Me as your Partner, than you would be with ten-tenths by yourself. For, you see, you do not live by your paycheck—you live by the blessings of God. You may have picked up your paycheck from your job, but if God did not wake you up this morning, what good is your paycheck? The issue is not the size of your paycheck; it is how you are blessed.

It would be so much easier for nontithers to become tithers if they understood and embraced the principle that one does not live by the paycheck—one lives by the blessings of God. If, for example, your paycheck is $1,000 and you did not tithe, but had $1,500 in medical bills, you have a deficit of $500. Nothing is left for yourself. Conversely, if your paycheck is $1,000 and you return $100 tithe, God may bless you so you did not get sick, then you still have $900 for yourself. So, it is never how much money you make—it is always how much you are blessed. And God says, Remove the barriers and the blessings will flow; return to Me My tithe and I will open the windows of heaven and pour you out a blessing so that there will not be room enough to receive it.

Tithing is God's plan

Tithing is not a human plan—it is God's plan. It is a sacred, simple, and satisfying plan. God expects it. God explains it. God encourages it. The *first* reason we bring the tithe is because we understand the commandment.

But there is a *second* reason why we bring the tithe. Turn with me to 2 Chronicles 31:11, 12: "Then Hezekiah commanded to prepare chambers in the house of the LORD; and they prepared them, and brought in the offerings and *the tithes* and the dedicated things faithfully" (emphasis added). These verses are climactic to a series of reforms that had taken place under King Hezekiah. Hezekiah was a godly king who led the nation in the greatest spiritual revivals. He opened the house of the Lord that his father had closed, cleansed the land of the false gods the people had been worshiping, reinstituted the feast and festival days, and started offering sacrifices and burnt offerings again. The Bible says that when the burnt offerings were made, the sight, smell, and sound began a revival; the people consecrated themselves and brought the tithe unto the Lord. Why did they bring the tithe? They brought the tithe because they understood consecration.

A good sign of the consecration of a Christian is bringing tithe to the house of the Lord. You see, the tithe is not just one-tenth of our income—it is an expression of the dedication of all of our income. When we bring the 10 percent, we acknowledge God's Lordship over 100 percent. We are saying, "Lord, I want to use the other nine-tenths to glorify You. All that I have and ever hope to be, I consecrate to You." Why do we bring the tithe? Because we understand consecration.

We are stewards of everything and owners of nothing. In order to remind us that we are stewards over everything and owners of nothing, God always reserves a portion for Himself. He says, You are stewards over six days, but the seventh day belongs to Me. Likewise, you are stewards over nine-tenths of your income, but one-tenth belongs to Me. And when we do not give God His portion, God collects it in His way.

Do you remember how God told Israel to work the fields, but that a portion of the field belonged to Him? God instructed them to rest every seventh year the portion that belonged to Him. But what did Israel do? The people worked the fields for 490 years and did not rest God's portion for one single year. You divide 490 years by seven and that means that God had seventy years of soil rest coming—and God collected it! When they went into bondage, how long were they captive in Babylonia? Seventy years. Second Chronicles 36:21 states that they were held in captivity "until the land had enjoyed her sabbaths [rest]." God had seventy years of soil rest coming, and He collected it.

Beloved, we can wear God's tithe on our backs, drive God's tithe to work, spend God's tithe on vacation, use God's tithe for tuition or to pay our monthly bills—but God will collect His tithe. God says, Give Me the portion that belongs to Me—or you are cursed with a curse. Sometimes when we file for bankruptcy, lie sick on a hospital bed, or stand in the unemployment line, it is because we are cursed with a curse. For our sake, we can never put God in second place—God will not allow that. So the second reason we bring the tithe is because we understand consecration.

But there is a *third* reason why we bring the tithe to the Lord. Turn with me to Genesis 28:22. Jacob is fleeing from his brother, Esau, because Esau threatened to chop off his head. He comes to Haran at nightfall and uses a rock for his pillow and spends the night in fitful dreaming. He saw that God had constructed a ladder that could get folks from earth to heaven. Jacob woke up the next morning, a thoroughly converted young man.

Genesis 28:20–22 tells us that Jacob made a covenant with God. Up until this point in his life, his philosophy was to get, get, get. This is what got him in trouble with his brother in the first place: get his brother's birthright; get his brother's blessing; get his brother's benefits! That is why many nontithers do not bring the tithe because of the "get" syndrome—get another dress; get another car; get another house—get, get, get! But when Jacob met God, his life was changed. Jacob proclaimed, "Of all that thou shalt give me I will surely give the tenth unto thee" (Genesis 28:22). His conversion changed the *get* syndrome into the *give* syndrome. Why did he bring the tithe? *He brought the tithe because he finally understood conversion.* Do you understand conversion, what it means to be saved? You see, you are saved because of a gift—"God so loved the world, that he gave his only begotten Son" (John 3:16). Jesus loved us so much that He *gave* Himself. And you cannot accept the gift of a Savior and yet not love Him ten cents' worth out of every dollar. Why do we bring the tithe? We bring the tithe because we understand conversion.

An unconverted pocketbook is an index to an unconverted heart. God does not want the gift—He wants the giver. God does not want the tithe—He wants the tither. God does not want your money—He wants you! Jesus did not die for your money—He died for you. Jesus knows that when He has you, He will have your money. And if He does not have your money, it is because He does not have *you*!

Do you remember the story of Jesus' encounter with Zacchaeus (Luke 19:1–10)? While walking under a sycamore tree, Jesus said to Zacchaeus, "Come down, I'm going to eat dinner at your house today." After Jesus came to his house, Zacchaeus was never the same again. Zacchaeus was converted that day; and before Jesus left, Zacchaeus said to Jesus, "The half of my goods, I give to the poor." The first proof of his conversion was his willingness to give. Zacchaeus said, I'm starting out, not just with 10 percent, but I'm going to give up to 50 percent. And watch what Jesus said to Zacchaeus, "This day has salvation come to your house." We are not saved because we give—we give because we are saved. We do not tithe in order to be saved—we tithe because we are saved. So the third reason we bring the tithe is because we understand conversion.

There is a *fourth* reason that we bring the tithe. Turn to Genesis 14:18, where we find the first mention of tithing. The first mention of any subject in the Bible is very important because it gives us the key to its importance. In Genesis 14, we are told Abraham rescued his nephew Lot out of the hands of the king of Elam. On the way back home, he met two kings. One was the king of Sodom, who said to Abraham, Give me. But, there was also the king of Salem, Melchizedek, priest of the Most High God. And what does he do? Scripture says in Genesis 14:18 that when he came out to meet Abraham, Melchizedek brought *bread and wine*. What did that mean? We know from reading the book of Hebrews that Melchizedek was a type of Christ. So a type of Christ comes out to meet Abraham, and what does he have in his hand? He has *bread and wine.*

You see, Old Testament Abraham in that distant land looked forward by faith to the Cross; and in that bread and wine, he saw the body and blood of Christ. Genesis 14:20 says that Abraham gave Melchizedek tithe of all that he possessed. Abraham looked forward and, by faith, saw Calvary. The very next thing the Bible says is that he gave his tithe. Why did he give the tithe? He brought the tithe because he understood Calvary. We, too, bring the tithe because we understand Calvary. For what Abraham looked forward to by *faith,* you and I look back to as a historical *fact.*

We look backward and see Christ with His broken body and blood poured out for us on a hill called Calvary. And the Christian says, Did He do that for me? He died in agony upon the cruel cross, covered with blood and spit and shame, for me? He suffered as no one else has ever been called upon to suffer, for me? The very least that I can do is to bring the tithe. So the fourth reason we bring the tithe is because we understand Calvary.

Prove Me now

Remember the words of Malachi that say, "Prove Me now." You can hear testimonies of those who tithe faithfully and hear of the blessings they experience. But you will never know the full blessing until you put God to the test. I challenge you today, not for my sake or the sake of this church, but for your sake. You are the one who will win or lose. You have been thinking, praying, and struggling with it for a long time, but you have never taken that step of faith—put God to the test.

Tell the Lord that you will put Him to the test for six months; and if He fails you, *you* will quit tithing. But, if God keeps His promise, be a faithful tither. God is willing if you are willing. And at the end of six months, if God failed you, I will give you an opportunity to give your testimony before this entire congregation and tell everybody how God failed you. God says to you, Put Me to the test and see how I will bless you.

Prove me *now*—not next week, next month, or next year! Start right *now*! Go home today and get down on your knees and claim Malachi 3:10. And for the next six months, come to the Lord's house bringing the Lord's tithe on the Lord's day and see if the Lord will not do what He says He will do.

Why do we bring the tithe? We bring the tithe because we understand the command. We bring the tithe because we understand consecration. We bring the tithe because we understand conversion. We bring the tithe because we understand Calvary. Do you really understand Calvary?

Do you understand Calvary as Frances Ridley Havergal understood Calvary? Listen to the words of her classic hymn

"I Gave My Life for Thee." Jesus is speaking directly to you when He says,

> I gave my life for thee,
> My precious blood I shed,
> That thou might'st ransomed be,
> And quickened from the dead;
> I gave, I gave My life for thee,
> What hast thou given for Me?[2]

What have *you* given for Christ? How much is Christ worth to you? Is He worth as much as a dime out of every dollar? How much have you given to Him? Do you understand Calvary?

Endnotes

1. Unless otherwise noted, all biblical quotations are from the King James Version.

2. Frances Ridley Havergal, "I Gave My Life for Thee," *The Seventh-day Adventist Hymnal* (Hagerstown, Md.: Review and Herald®, 1985), no. 281.

Can't Buy Love

Harold O. White

I want to tell you a story from my childhood in Anthon, a small town in western Iowa. It's really a story about my dad, a grocery store, and baseball. When my brother, Gary, and I were growing up in that town, there were no organized baseball teams for the children. My brother and I liked baseball, and so Dad, along with some others, organized teams for the children. Dad wanted his boys to have an opportunity to play baseball. He put in tireless hours to get the teams going.

Dad got the boys together, obtained the needed equipment, and worked hard preparing the town baseball diamond. Finally, he took on the additional task of coaching the team. He really did not want to be the coach, but he did it until they found another person to fill that role. My parents enthusiastically did whatever it took to keep the teams going. In order to raise the needed funds, they started a snack shack to sell food at the games. In order to get the children to the games, Dad picked up kids, took them home, and helped provide for their uniforms. Dad and Mom did whatever was needed to make the teams an enjoyable experience for the children.

The disappointment

Then one night, my father experienced a big disappointment. As I said, he owned a little grocery store on Main Street. On winter nights, he would stop at the store before retiring for the night and check the furnace. On this particular evening, he entered the front door and walked to the back of the store without turning on any lights. There was enough light from the street light for him to walk to the back of the store. Once he reached the back of the store, he reached into the little restroom and turned on the light before proceeding downstairs to check the furnace.

Then something unexpected happened. As he reached around the corner to turn on the light switch, his hand did not find the switch. Instead his hand landed on someone's face. It turned out to be a boy's face.

My dad's hand touched one boy's face, but soon he discovered that there were two boys hiding in the restroom. Both he and the boys were startled. What were two boys whom he had helped doing there? The realization was painful—they had broken into the store in order to steal cigarettes and other appealing items. Once they heard my father coming into the store, they hid. My father was disappointed that some of the young people for whom he had done so much would rob him. How would you have felt if someone for whom you had done much robbed you?

What about us?

Robbery unfortunately occurs all too often. It's not only children who rob those who do good things for them. Adults rob each other; stealing even occurs within families. Taking what does not belong to us all too often even involves taking from God. The Bible uses blunt language to describe our acts against God. In Malachi 3:8, we are asked, " 'Will a mere mortal rob God? Yet you rob me' " (NIV). Think of it. God gives, God blesses, and then He asks for only a tenth to be reserved for Him. He asks for offerings, but He leaves it up to us to decide how much to give. God makes an easy to understand request—if we earn $100, God asks for us to return $10 in tithe.

I've had people ask this question: Do you mean to tell me that God expects me to give to Him one-tenth of all that I make? They seem to be implying that it is unreasonable for God to ask for us to return tithe. But remember, God is asking us to return to Him only a *portion* of what He has given. First, He blesses, and then He asks us to be faithful and return only a portion of that. And why does God ask us to return tithe? We do not return tithe because He needs our money. We return it to show faithfulness to Him. When we are faithful to God, He repeats the cycle—He blesses us again. The cycle of blessing and faithfulness continues. Thus, returning tithe is a spiritual experience.

When I first was thinking about becoming a Christian, the concept of tithing made sense to me. I began returning tithe quite a while before I was baptized. Why did it make so much sense? I'm not one of those gifted financial geniuses, who turns everything into gold, so I thought going into partnership with God was the safest plan for financial security. But I didn't understand the tithing concept completely. The church my wife, Dorreen, and I were attending, and eventually baptized in, was in the middle of a major renovation project. We had to step around piles of debris to get to a pew. The church was a construction site. So, of course, the church made appeals for funds needed for the renovation. About that time, I had some money come to me that was above my regular salary. We were happy to have some extra money to give to the building program. I took the money that should have been the tithe on that income, added some more and turned it in for the renovation project. I did not return the tithe, but I gave an offering.

A few weeks later, I was riding a tractor on a farm owned

by one of the church elders. He told me the church was happy to receive our financial support even though we were not yet members. I explained where the extra money came from and that my wife and I were really excited about supporting the building project. When I explained the whole situation—the extra income, not returning tithe but giving offerings—he didn't seem to share my excitement. It wasn't until later that I found out why. I had not returned tithe, but I had used tithe money for a building program. There are many wonderful causes in the world. Multitudes of worthy projects vie for our attention, and building or renovating a church is one of them. But God says that the tithe is to be used for special purposes and not as an offering.

Numbers 18:21 tells us how the tithe is to be used. It states, "Behold, I have given the children of Levi all the tenth in Israel for an inheritance, for their service which they serve, even the service of the tabernacle of the congregation" (KJV). Those who ministered to God's people were to receive the tithe.

The apostle Paul in 1 Corinthians 9:13, 14 also tells us the purpose of tithe, for he writes, "Do ye not know that they which minister about holy things live of the things of the temple? and they which wait at the altar are partakers with the altar? Even so hath the Lord ordained that they which preach the gospel should live of the gospel" (KJV). The Bible is clear about the purpose of tithe. It is set apart for ministry, for the proclamation of the good news about God. Ellen White tells us in a few well-chosen words that tithe funds "should not in any case be devoted to any other use."[1]

Don't try to make God too small

If we ignore the Word of God, it's easy to argue that tithe may be used for other purposes. I think we can come up with wrong conclusions because we have some wrong concepts about God and what He said. A Bible scholar, J. B. Phillips writes, "Many people, including many Christians have wildly inaccurate ideas about who God is. They perceive Him as Resident Policeman, Parental Hangover, Grand Old Man, The Meek and Mild One, The Managing Director, The Man Upstairs, The Pale Galilean, and many others. All of these reflect a God who is not the God of the Bible, and a Jesus who is much too small."[2] Indeed, our concept of God affects our stewardship. If a person thinks God is a Santa Claus–type figure—one who only gives, but does not accept anything from us—that person's view of stewardship is warped. God indeed gives, but He wants us to act as responsible stewards also.

At the same time, we must not fear God. I recall another incident that occurred shortly after I started attending church. One of the church members said to me, "On that day, *that glorious day,* when Jesus returns and brightens the sky with all His glory, accompanied by millions of shining angels; on that day, I wouldn't want one thin dime of God's money in my pocket." It's not fear that makes us faithful stewards—faithfulness makes us faithful stewards.

Stewardship is about choice

Some years ago, the Beatles sang a song called "Can't Buy Me Love."[3] Actually, you can't buy love from anyone. Perhaps for a large sum of money I may *like* you, but I would not truly love you. In the same way, you can't buy God's love. The good news is that you don't *need* to buy God's love. God loves us always. Period. Thus, if you or I return a tithe or give offering as a way of "getting" God's love, we have the wrong concept of stewardship.

Biblical stewardship is about choices—the choices that we make. I am reminded about the Sabbath School teacher who asked the children whether they would give one million dollars to the missionaries, if they had that money.

"Yes!" they all screamed.

Then the teacher asked if they had $1,000 whether they would give it.

Again, they shouted an enthusiastic "Yes!"

How about $100 dollars? And you know how they responded again—yes, they would give the $100.

"And would you give a dollar for the work of the missionaries?" asked the teacher. Yes, they would give a dollar—that is all except one child.

"And why would you not give a dollar?" asked the teacher.

"Well," the child responded, "I *have* a dollar and I don't want to give it up."

That youngster was responding the way many respond. We promise to give what we don't have, but all too often we choose to not give that which we have. I can't tell you how many people have told me that if they came into some money, they'd give a big amount of the money to various ministries of the church.

"If I received a large amount of money," some say, "I will give it to help God's work." But what about that which we have? Are you a faithful steward of that which you possess?

I was studying the Bible with a young couple in Indiana. Early in our studies the man told me that he would never give up drinking beer. Every night after coming home from work, he told me, he would drink one or two beers. He simply was not ready to give it up. I assured him that I was not capable of taking his beer from him. Sometime later when I came for another Bible study, he announced he had quit drinking beer. It was a choice that he, under the guidance of the Holy Spirit, had made. He chose to be a good steward of his body. Only after he had made the choice to stop drinking did he realize how addictive his drinking had become.

We continued the studies and ran into something else he was not prepared to do. After we studied about tithe and offerings, he told me he would not return the tithe and give offerings.

This man worked in graphic design for a large company. For many years he also tried to establish his own sign business on the side. He possessed good skills and occasionally would get orders for signs. One day after our continued studies, he made the decision to start tithing. Again, he listened to the guidance of the Holy Spirit. And then he told me what happened. The week he turned in his first tithe, his private sign business took off like a rocket and, within a couple of years, he retired from his employer, even though he was still a young man. He worked full time making signs. His new business grew so rapidly that he had to hire other people to work for him. This man, who once did not want to stop drinking beer or return a tithe and give offerings, became a church leader. He personally experienced the blessing Jesus promises in Luke 6:38: "Give, and it will be given to you. A good measure, pressed down, shaken together and running over, will be poured into your lap. For with the measure you use, it will be measured to you" (NIV). Faithful stewards are partners with God.

I am sure that you know people who have had similar experiences. Perhaps you have had such an experience. Whenever, under the guidance of the Holy Spirit, we choose to be faithful stewards, God blesses us. I am not promoting some kind of Bible sweepstakes, a get-rich-quick scheme, or some version of the so-called prosperity gospel. It's a matter of faithfulness; it's a matter of stewardship.

Let me share with you an experience our family had. Our boys wanted to get into the puppy raising business. They didn't have any money to start their business, so they devised all kinds of ways to earn it. One of our church elders asked them to paint his house. They wanted to accept, but they were too young to do it on their own. In order to help our sons, I agreed to help them on my days off, and soon they earned enough money to buy one male and three female cocker spaniels. They were thrilled when one of the females had six or seven cute puppies. We lived near one of the major thoroughfares of the city, and the hand-painted sign the boys made attracted potential buyers. Our sons were jubilant, as the puppies were soon sold. As young as they were, they had learned to be good stewards, for they returned tithe from their sales and kept the profits.

Later one afternoon, I came home just to get something to eat before going out again for my evening appointments.

"Here, Dad," one of them said, and they handed me a bag. "This is our gift to you for all the help you gave us to get our dog business started."

They watched anxiously as I opened the bag in which I found the best baseball glove that money could buy in those days. Before they took money from their little dog business, they first returned tithe. Then they gave me a gift to thank me for getting them started. It was one of the most exciting and memorable gifts I have ever received. I gained a new understanding and appreciation of Paul's words, "God loveth a cheerful giver" (2 Corinthians 9:7, KJV). It does us no good to give if it is not done cheerfully. Imagine how I would have felt if I knew the boys gave me the glove because they felt they had to do it. How fulfilling would it have been if I knew they had to be coaxed to give something? It's the same with us—we can't give cheerfully until we really get to know the Giver of all good things. That's faithful stewardship.

This I learned

Tithing and giving of offerings is not just a doctrine about money. It is one of the greatest demonstrations of what kind of love we have for God. But it was God who first gave—He gave His only begotten Son. Just as my boys were not forced to give me the glove, God was not forced to give His Son. He *chose* to give His Son Jesus as a gift.

I know that money can touch sensitive nerves in all of us. But friends, so did those nails and that crown of thorns touch sensitive nerves—very sensitive nerves in our dear Savior.

Someone asked me once, "You mean to tell me that I